LO

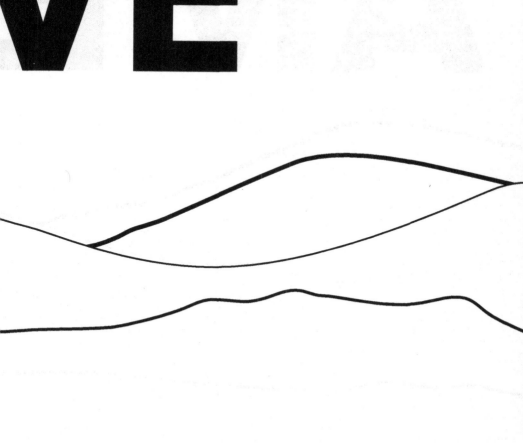

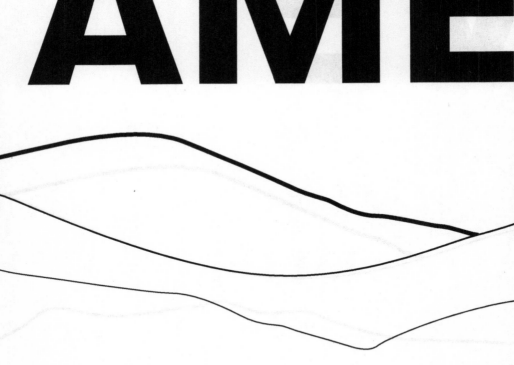

RICA

LOVE AMERICA

On the Trail of
Writers & Artists
in New Mexico

JENNY ROBIN JONES

calico

Also by Jenny Robin Jones

Writers in Residence:
A Journey with Pioneer New Zealand Writers
Auckland University Press, Auckland, 2004

No Simple Passage:
The Journey of the 'London' to New Zealand,
1842 — a ship of hope
Random House New Zealand, Auckland, 2011

Not For Ourselves Alone:
Belonging in an Age of Loneliness
Saddleback, Wellington, 2018

Calico Publishing Ltd
2A Heywood Crescent
Epsom
Auckland 1023
New Zealand
www.calicopublishing.co.nz

© Jenny Robin Jones 2020

ISBN 978-1-877429-35-4

First published in 2020

A catalogue record for this book is available from
the National Library of New Zealand
Also available as an ebook

Editor: Geoff Walker
Interior and cover design: Carla Sy
Printed in New Zealand

For Ray

Contents

Contents

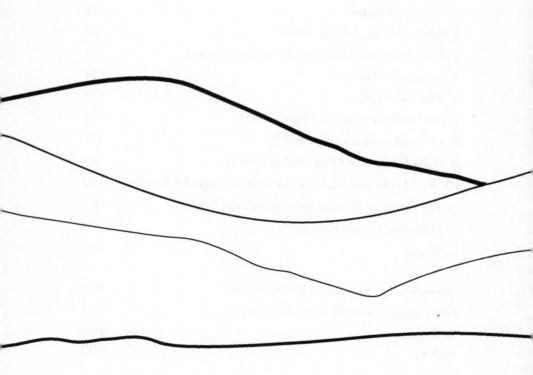

1
Ignition

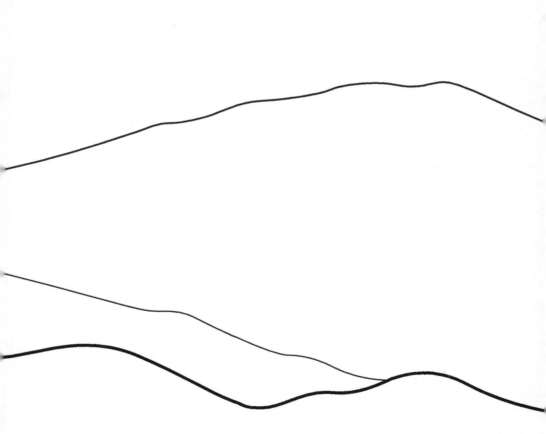

1

Ignition

E ach time the old man visited his son in San Francisco, he would add on a bit of travel in other parts of America, and by the time I knew him he had been doing this every year for thirty years. As he grew old each visit took a greater toll on his health until he toyed with giving up the visits. Then he became a grandfather. Two or three years later, Amelia could talk and Aidan was tottering across the lounge, but the o-m had still not seen them. As for me, I had never been to the States beyond a stopover and I longed to go with a person like the o-m. And one day I heard the magic words, Let's go.

The question was where. San Francisco obviously, but where else? Or was that all? No, the o-m wanted to make it a proper trip. Three weeks, say. He wanted to show me America. Of course he didn't mean all 9.8 million square kilometres of it, and anyway where was America? Years ago, the British show *Beyond the Fringe* had nailed the problem in a clever skit. Those catchy young men, Jonathan Miller, Alan Bennett and friends, profiled individual states, giving each its due but concluding, as we all have to, that nowhere in America represents America. Get that in your noddle and start again, Traveller!

The o-m's first suggestion was Los Angeles. Everything in me rebelled against it. Smoggy skies, glitz, superficiality, soullessness. I'd already been to Disneyland and didn't care if I never saw Universal Studios. I wanted to go somewhere on a human scale, somewhere rich in history, preferably associated with writers and literature. The o-m was in his eighties and already a little wearied by travel but he kindly came up with another suggestion – what about Taos and Santa Fe in New Mexico? I googled and was pleased by what I discovered:

> ➢ The population of Santa Fe was under 70,000 and that of Taos (rhymes with house) around 6000. In both places you could 'walk to everything' including the ancient pueblo still inhabited by Native Americans that gave Taos its name (human scale).
> ➢ In New Mexico the Spanish conquistadors had encountered Native American pueblos. Misunderstanding, bloody battles and exploitation had followed. Santa Fe was the first state capital in the United States (rich in history).
> ➢ Santa Fe and Taos were writers' colonies from 1917 to 1950. D H Lawrence (a blast from my teenage past) lived in Taos between 1922 and 1925. Willa Cather wrote one of my favourite American novels, *Death Comes for the Archbishop*, there (associated with writers and literature).

It was D H Lawrence who really fired my imagination about going to New Mexico. Writers' colonies had no special drawing power for me, but as a teenager I had read and responded to *Sons and Lovers*. I still remember the relationship between the narrator and his first love, Miriam. His dawning comprehension of the complexity and trauma of love. The terrible discomfort of both loving and hating the same person for reasons not fully understood. At university I read *Lady Chatterley's Lover*, as well as *Women in Love*, *The Rainbow*, short stories, essays and poetry. Reading *Lady C* I felt very grown up, especially when my mother asked me why people would want to *do* that with flowers (twine them in a woman's pubic hair). I loved the poetry, especially the animal ones, 'Snake', 'Mountain Lion'. I loved the language of Lawrence, his ability to create another world and transport me to it, a world that is an entity in itself but which can illuminate my own, especially my relationships and appreciation of beauty and ugliness.

I had not known much about Lawrence's personal life and somehow the idea of him having gone to New Mexico, and of my staying in the same house as he had, reconnected me with my adolescence. I would go to New Mexico, bringing that younger, impressionable self with me. If anyone was to take my hand in America, it would be Lawrence.

The o-m was amenable and we made our plans. Stopovers in Albuquerque and Santa Fe, three nights in Taos, one in Santa Fe and the rest in San Francisco where we'd spend Thanksgiving. The o-m undertook to research, book and pay for the accommodation. It was slightly awkward travelling together because our relationship had evolved into one where we did not have sex. Not because one or both of us did not want sex, but because we couldn't enjoy it together. Or, rather, I couldn't enjoy it with the o-m. We had started out with high hopes. His narrow single bed he would replace with a generous queen. The o-m loved style as well as comfort in his furniture, so we shopped around and lay on beds of many kinds. Our final choice allowed each person to move without affecting the other, but somehow sleeping together still didn't work, either at his place or mine. Supersensitive me lay awake hour after hour and even the segregated upholstery didn't save the o-m from being affected.

There was another problem. Following a normal human course, the o-m's body had reached a point where artificial assistance was necessary to fire it into action. That required pre-commitment, something I found as off-putting at this stage of my life as I had found the rhythm method when married to a Catholic. And then I found that even in touching there was incompatibility. One day on a long beach he had taken my hand but my fingers couldn't make space to be comfortable within his grasp and after a while I had to free myself. We loved each other and wanted to be together, but all we could really achieve physically was a peck on the lips.

So, what to do about accommodation? We couldn't afford single rooms and perhaps, too, we didn't want to advertise failure, so I suggested twin beds and the o-m agreed. He researched diligently, but sometimes only a double bed was on offer. Once, after a particularly gruelling online session, he told me what he had booked, grumbling, Don't worry, you'll have your single beds. Generous in victory, I kept my mouth shut.

Actually the o-m had excelled himself. The accommodation in Taos was a building that had been for many decades the centre for a writers' and artists' colony. It was where Lawrence came to stay on his first visit and where Cather had written her novel. Lawrence had painted the windows of one of the bathrooms and, nearly a hundred years later, they survived.

Next, the o-m turned his attention to transport within the States. Driving not an option: the o-m's reaction times too slow and me too timid to claim the right-hand side on leaving the airport. Public transport was neither frequent nor direct, but the o-m came up with trains and buses and found accommodation he told me was within walking distance of stations.

As it turned out, the New Mexico section of the trip proved the most exciting and revelatory and was the only part I wanted to write about. It changed my feeling about America, gave me a sense of deep connection with it, offered a way out of my climate-change dilemma about flying and ultimately brought me together with the o-m in a way I'd never thought possible.

All my life the idea of America had occupied a space in my psyche. Its very formation was a body blow to Great Britain, where I grew up. My first ideas of it were formed through watching Westerns. The land was defined by the people, the wild cowboys fighting the scalping Indians. Wolves and coyotes were things to be shot at with guns. The land never existed by itself or for itself. Buffalo, deer, the weather, the cold, the heat — it was all something to conquer. This was all so much a part of my growing up that I never consciously thought about it.

My second impression was of America as a place of stupendous wealth and materialism. It was crass, its comedies were predictable, it boasted of itself interminably, it was people waving their Stars & Stripes at every opportunity, jazz, rock 'n' roll, country and western, big American presidents, limos, Hollywood stars. As I grew older I realised America brimmed with missionary zeal towards the rest of the world. It believed it had a right to bend others to its own view, especially in relation to democracy and economy. In recent years it had caused more and more chaos around the world and was even now continuing on its wrecking-ball path. I needed to see it. I needed to find a way to live with it and not despair. I needed to update my idea of America.

The journey raised many questions and I returned with a sense of compulsion to find the answers. Much of my normal life at home is conducted in conditions of voluntary lockdown, so I read many books, both fiction and non-fiction, and slowly began to feel at ease with what I had seen. Afterwards I realised that I had been offered a different way of travelling. The travel was not just the journey itself but the attempt to make sense of it afterwards. One short trip could supply a year or so of fruitful enquiry. Meanwhile there was the daily news. America was still behaving like a bully, so what did I make of that now I had been there? How had the journey changed me?

This is not an attempt to write more than what I have seen. Like a game of roulette, chance brought before me Lawrence, Cather, Taos Pueblo, Mabel and Tony Luhan, Millicent Rogers Museum, Georgia O'Keeffe. The places where the dice deposited me contained grains of sand in which I could see, if I took the trouble, America.

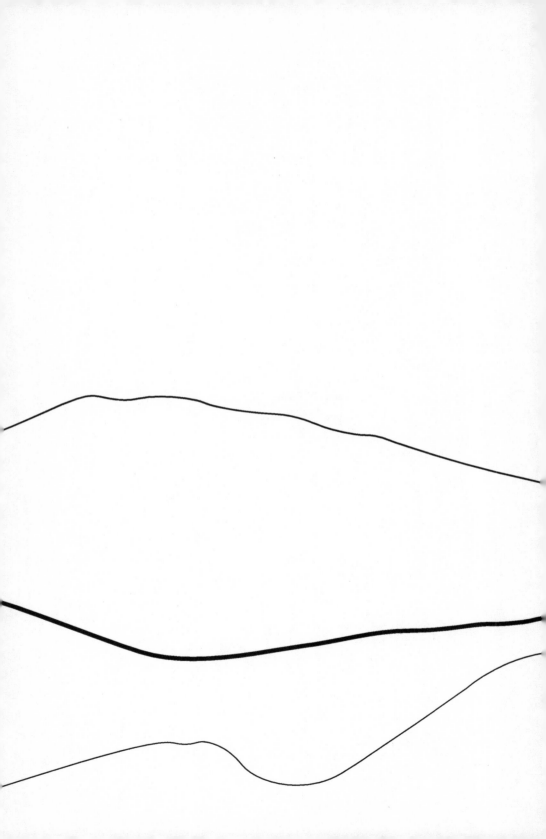

2
The Big House

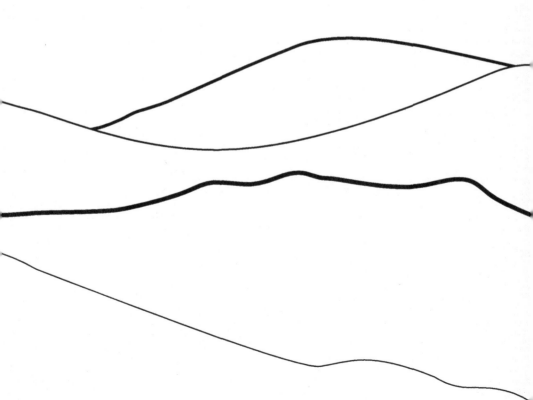

2

The Big House

First stop was LA, where we went through airport formalities with astonishing speed and walked into a world featuring a natural blue sky. This was not what I had been led to expect. Silly me. I had arrived staggering under the weight of my stereotypes and now hastened to dismantle them. Of course the sky would *sometimes* be blue, not *all* bus depots were dangerous, I'd *probably* get home without having been shot. The flight attendant on our flight to New Mexico had dazzling-white, flawlessly even teeth. 'A classic American smile,' the o-m said. It should have seemed like a natural wonder, but it did not.

At Albuquerque airport, while we waited for the man at the information desk to phone our hotel and book us a courtesy car, the o-m noticed a battered jacket lying on a chair and set in play his powers of deduction. One of the patches sown into the jacket showed the man had been a naval aviator, another identified the aircraft carrier he had flown on. That made things easy for the o-m, who had once spent an entire morning examining the carrier in the San Francisco Bay area. The o-m popped the question and the man at the desk confirmed. Yes, he was a Vietnam War vet. He stood straighter as he told the o-m what he'd flown in Nam and the o-m told him about his naval aviator friend who had flown Corsairs in World War II. Corsairs were beyond my comprehension, the word made me think of Cossacks. I began looking at brochures.

I would like to have asked different questions, questions that came to my mind from watching the news. How was he treated on returning as a veteran? Did he suffer post-traumatic stress disorder? How did he cope? What were his feelings now about that war? Even to myself I sounded like a sociological investigator. As a military historian, the o-m respected what soldiers did. He didn't need to ask a lot of questions.

The next morning we walked down to Albuquerque's Old Town, seeing on the way an astonishing number of law offices, a courthouse, a bail bonds building and pawn shops. It seemed as though the people in this place engaged in nothing but lawsuits and gaol time. Judging by the number of hair salons, they also enjoyed having their hair done.

A painting at the Albuquerque Museum offered the first intimation of personalities who would feature in my literary pilgrimage: Lawrence, his wife Frieda and his patron Mabel Dodge Luhan, progenitor of our accommodation in Taos. Also Dorothy Brett, creator of the painting and adoring fan of Lawrence. She came to visit Lawrence in New Mexico, believing in his dream of establishing a utopian community, and stayed for the rest of her life.

The o-m was not overly interested in literary pilgrimage but art fascinated him, so together we examined the painting. The three women were seated around a table, Mabel looking business-like and in charge, Frieda at the head, smoking.

Brett, as she was known, even by friends, sat tentative before her typewriter while Lawrence perched on a bench some distance behind them all, as if suspended in space, his face turned away. The painting was called *My Three Fates*. Brett painted it in 1958, many years after Lawrence's death.

In the afternoon we gathered up our belongings to catch a Rail Runner to Santa Fe. I discovered that the o-m's 'walking distance' between hotels and transport could mean a kilometre or two and it was not so easy on streets of uneven camber to wheel both a suitcase and a carry-on. At the station, we talked to a man who commuted to the city for work. He was sad that Albuquerque, despite its metropolitan population of nearly a million, couldn't afford a football team. An Amtrak train whooshed in, people surged forward, and the o-m, who had wandered down the platform, fantasised that when the crowd dispersed, I would have vanished. He would approach the man who dreamed of a football team for his city. Where is she? he would demand and the guy would answer, Who? The o-m loved movies, Hitchcock a perennial favourite. Five minutes in America and already I was in a gangster movie.

On the Rail Runner some recent news came back to me with acid regurgitation, a report that the US was averaging one mass shooting per day. I looked around at my fellow passengers. Who had a finger near a trigger? I forced myself to be sensible and look at the desert and notice the casinos on the reservations. What a lot of cottonwood and sagebrush. The o-m nudged me, wanting to impart more information. 'This is Los Alamos. The first atomic bomb was tested here in 1945.' The o-m knew much more and would have shared, but perhaps I didn't want to know, perhaps this wasn't what I had come for. Enough to know I was at the cradle of the atomic bomb, technology that could have ended the world and still might. The vulnerability of desert. A place where things can be hidden.

The Rail Runner ran from Albuquerque to Santa Fe,

and the end of the line, when we reached it, brooked no argument. We alighted on an apology for a platform and walked beside the track for a few metres before it gave up, cowed by two uncompromising buffers, beyond them a road. It was too dark to read a map and very cold. Our hotel, booked with a pleasant stroll in mind, was now on the other side of a menacing unknown.

As we dithered, a man emerged from the blackness and asked if he could help. He was waiting for a bus to the Buffalo Thunder Casino somewhere on the road north, likely a croupier or waiter, but the sight of us two shivering in the dark worried him. He rang our hotel for a courtesy car and when this was refused he gave us walking directions. We could hear the worry in his voice. He sent us on our way with a handshake, I've heard New Zealand is paradise — but no tips! and a warning, A lot of crooks in this country — be wise. How many of his 320 million fellow countrymen would he class as crooks, I wondered. How hard must it be to feel safe here?

I dragged my suitcase along the pavement, swivelled my eyes front-back-and-sides, held my handbag tightly, hoped the journey would not be long. I began to understand the ubiquitous flags and the at-the-ready patriotism. America the greatest, the greatest, the greatest. Methinks she doth protest too much.

Beneath the greatness, the insecurity. How can 320 million people, spread over 9.8 million square kilometres, belong together? How can there be such a thing as 'American values'? You'd just have to fly the same flag all over the country and nurture external enemies and insist that your country's dream was the best, and pray God bless America and hope He would. I said as much to the o-m who said, No other country of such size even attempts to run a democracy.

We found the hotel. A not-quite-standard Hilton with welcoming open fire and sofas in the lobby. Apart from sampling a Mexican meal we saw nothing of Santa Fe because our bus left early next day for Taos. The fare was free on weekdays but the bus was rickety with hard seats, not built for people with expectations. The o-m told me that much of the land we were seeing was Indian reservation and that one of the few ways Native Americans could generate income was by running casinos for the outside population. This struck me as sad. Sad in the way that a white person living a comfortable, purposeful life thinks sad.

I felt disconnected from Native Americans. Out of the window I saw none. Just sagebrush and cottonwood. Cottonwood and sagebrush. The more I stared the less I understood, but I have never been any good at describing scenery. Often I feel as if I don't even see it properly until I feel connected with it, but when that happens I can't describe it either, because what I feel then is too intimate to reduce to words. At least I was being confronted with America as a physical entity instead of as a sort of giant amoeba for politicians to gambol over. Even American novels hadn't enabled me to transmogrify contour and landscape into rocks and trees in a physical country.

By the time we reached Taos we were over 2000 metres above sea level. We had been warned to drink plenty of water and be careful when walking. Already we hadn't been careful, lugging our cases uphill on an unsealed road, carrying them over cobblestones and steps. The skin on my fingers became paper thin within hours and I had to apply sticking plasters to avoid open wounds.

As soon as I saw the hotel, I felt a sense of coming home. A house built with love, bursting with dreams. Traditional Pueblo design and materials had gone into its construction — thick adobe walls heaped storey upon storey, like tiers on a wedding cake, each smaller in circumference than the last, the lowest level supported by huge adobe buttresses. This was the Big House. Come in, it said to me, make yourself at home (breakfast is free and fragrant, home-made cookies served all day). Around the Big House were several small houses, also open for guests, that dated back to the 1920s. Also a much newer building that incorporated a large classroom.

The o-m had booked us into the Big House and chosen the Cather Room. Not the Frieda Lawrence Room or the O'Keeffe Room, the Ansel Adams Room, the Dorothy Brett Room, Frank Waters Room or Mabel's or Tony's rooms, but the Cather Room, because I loved the novels of Willa Cather and because she had worked on *Death Comes for the Archbishop* right here.

And there was another link. About a year ago, the o-m had lent me *Not Under Forty*, a book of essays about things Cather (rhyme it with 'gather') deemed would interest no one under that age. In one chapter, she wrote about Katherine Mansfield and even singled out one of my own favourite stories, 'The Doll's House', praising its magical touch in evoking a family from Mansfield's New Zealand childhood. She says the very letters on the page become alive. She also includes an essay about an elderly man who met Mansfield on a crossing to Australia when she was a child. Katherine adopted him for the voyage and he enjoyed her conversation immensely.

The Cather Room had twin beds, but there was a problem even now. Everywhere we went, people would make assumptions about us that were not true and our silence would be a kind of deceit. The o-m and I never discussed this. We had solved the problem insofar as we were able and the case was closed. The o-m must have been aware of the missignalling we were complicit in and, like me, decided it didn't really matter.

There was a small table in the Cather Room where, I was told, Cather worked on her novel, and a small open fire for perishingly cold winter nights. The room overflowed with character and was therefore slightly inconvenient but we loved it. I discovered later that Cather stayed only two weeks at Mabel's and that was in the Pink House.

No matter. Though she was never drawn to move to New Mexico, it had a profound influence on both her and her work, as I discovered after my return home. She first visited the Southwest in 1912, staying with her brother who worked for the Santa Fe Railway and also in Albuquerque. Her time there, which was recuperative, allowed her to immerse herself in the grand overarching scale of the geology, riding and following other whims, which included witnessing the ritual Hopi Snake Dance. She had not been so happy since she was a child.

This experience changed Cather's understanding of land and the way she wrote about it forever. She grasped as if for the first time the profound interconnections between land and the people who lived and worked on it. The first novel to reflect her new understanding was her masterpiece *O Pioneers!*, which gave her readers an insider's feeling about the plains country of her homeland Nebraska and the European immigrants who struggled to tame it. In the second, *The Song of the Lark*, she presented what were probably her own feelings about the Southwest through the thoughts of the heroine, Thea Kronborg,

> The personality of which she was so tired seemed to let go of her. The high sparkling air drank it up like blotting-paper. It was lost in the thrilling blue of the new sky and the song of the thin wind in the piñons. The old, fretted lines which marked one off, which defined her – made her Thea Kronborg, Bower's accompanist, a soprano with a faulty middle voice – were all erased.[1]

On further visits Cather was fascinated by the bronze statue of Archbishop Lamy outside the Santa Fe cathedral, but it was not until 1925 when she read a book about Lamy's lifelong friend and assistant, Joseph Machebeuf, that she was inspired to write a novel about the friendship between the clerics. By then two remarkable women, Mary Austin and Mabel Dodge Luhan, had formed writers' colonies in Santa Fe and Taos respectively, which eased the logistics of writing so far from home.

Austin and Luhan were rivals in competition for the favours of writers and artists. At first Austin, an accomplished novelist and ethnographer, had made Mabel's home the headquarters for her research among northern pueblos, but as both women aimed to be accepted as women of genius and collectors of geniuses, it was probably inevitable that Austin would leave tiny Taos and set up her own colony in Santa Fe. From there, she would beckon to Cather.

Cather and her lifelong companion Edith Lewis were staying with Mary when Mabel invited them to Taos. Like the Lawrences before them, they were put up in the Pink House, and Cather found her time there so rewarding that she extended it to two weeks. She and Edith had met the Lawrences when they were in New York, where Lawrence had held them spellbound with tales of their time in Ceylon. He was especially brilliant at imitating the sounds of the leopards leaping on the roof of the bungalow and hunting for mice in the thatch. In Taos, the Lawrences made Willa and Edith welcome at their ranch.

While Willa and Edith were in the Pink House, Mabel was very sensitive to her guests' needs, leaving them alone except for meals which they ate at the Big House. Her husband, Tony Luhan, talked with Willa about the land and people of New Mexico and sang Pueblo songs to her. She liked him very much and it seems he became her model for Eusabio in *Death Comes for the Archbishop*, while Lamy and Machebeuf were the models for Archbishop Latour and Father Vaillant.

Mary Austin also found a way to assist. In 1926 she invited Willa to use her home while she was in hospital and Willa later inscribed her thanks in a copy of the novel for the use of her 'lovely study', where she wrote the last chapters of the book. The inscription also invited Austin to be her sternest critic. As befits a writers' colony, there has been disagreement about whether the inscription is genuine, because Cather later denied that she wrote any of the novel in the house. Perhaps, it was suggested, Austin's desire for Cather's reflected glory prompted her to forge it. However, while in Santa Fe Cather wrote to Austin saying how much she was enjoying writing her novel at her house. Then again, instead of mentioning the study, she wrote that she was working from the blue plush chair in a corner of the library, so it's possible the inscription was a forgery intended to show that Cather accepted Austin's critical role. Cather certainly didn't welcome the stern critic when she encountered her in Austin's autobiography.

My literary pilgrimage was under way, and before the day was out I prevailed upon the person at reception to let me go upstairs. With each step my heart quickened its beat and then there it was: a room with a claw-foot bath and every one of the eight windows painted by Lawrence! In bright Mexican colours, he had depicted aspects of Native American culture. Why did he do it? One of the walls overlooked the roof of the floor below, where Mabel liked to sunbathe. Some people thought that Lawrence wanted to avoid her nudity, or perhaps it was to protect her privacy within the room. Or his. The body and its meaning. According to Lawrence, nothing could be experienced without a degree of turmoil.

In fact he had not painted the windows by himself, but with Dorothy Brett, the artist whose painting of the Lawrences and Mabel I had seen in Albuquerque. Lawrence had met her in London and persuaded her to come to Taos to help further his dream of Rananim, where people would live together in harmony with the land.

Brett was the daughter of a viscount, used to moving in aristocratic and upper-class circles. Grandfather Brett was Queen Victoria's Master of the Rolls and a Lord Justice of the Court of Appeals. Her first date was with Winston Churchill, but she was a rebel by nature. Her sister Sylvia wrote that she 'scorned the ritual of matchmaking, snubbed her escorts, and as soon as the parties were over, cut off her hair, dressed like a boy, and became one of the best-known figures in the painters' pubs in Chelsea'.[2]

Brett first met Lawrence in 1915. She had recently met Katherine Mansfield and John Middleton Murry. At the time she had fallen in love with Lady Ottoline Morrell, the famous inspiration for Hermione in *Women in Love*. Ottoline invited Brett to her country estate at Garsington, where she met Aldous and Julian Huxley, Bertrand Russell, Virginia and Leonard Woolf, Lytton Strachey and the rest of the Bloomsbury group, and there too she came to know Katherine and Murry well. She regarded Katherine as her dearest friend and swore a pact of eternal friendship with her. The friendship survived Brett's short affair with Murry and it was Brett who Katherine turned to for support at the end of her life. It was through Brett that she met Gurdjieff and finally went to Fontainebleau for spiritual healing.

Meanwhile, Lawrence and Frieda had been to India and Australia and had spent the winter of 1922-23 with Mabel in Taos. In April 1924 they again travelled, this time to Mexico and New York. By the end of August, Frieda was back in England and Lawrence on his way back to Mexico via California. It was an open question whether Lawrence would join Frieda again or not. Then they were both back in London, prior to returning to Taos, meeting up with Brett again and Lawrence begging Brett to come. Although

Rananim did not work out, Brett devoted the rest of her life to Lawrence. After his death she continued to live and paint in Taos until her death at ninety-four. By then she had lived longer at Mabel's place than any of the other artists and writers who came, so it is fitting that to this day she has a presence there. Guests may stay if they choose in the Dorothy Brett room and have a view of the guesthouse where Lawrence and Frieda stayed and which is now called the D H Lawrence House.

I returned to find the o-m had fallen asleep so I lay down too. As I stared through the window at Cather's writing view, I was reminded of that Mansfield story 'The Doll's House'. The part where the working-class child, Else, finally gets to see the doll's house of her upper-class schoolmates. She has been craving to see it ever since the other girls started talking about it, but of course she was not invited to look. At last one of its owners takes pity on her. The thing Else loves the most is a little amber lamp with a white globe that was all filled ready for lighting. Her precious memory, 'I seen the little lamp', said everything about the fulfilment of reaching a destination against the odds. And here I was in Cather's Room, where I then believed an author I loved wrote a novel I loved, and on the storey above was Lawrence, decorating the bathroom windows. Of course I thought of the story.

It was as if I had come to a museum and touched living people. The hem of Jesus's robe. Stardust falling on my jeans. Was this what I had come for? Only this?

3

Adobe Here,
Adobe There

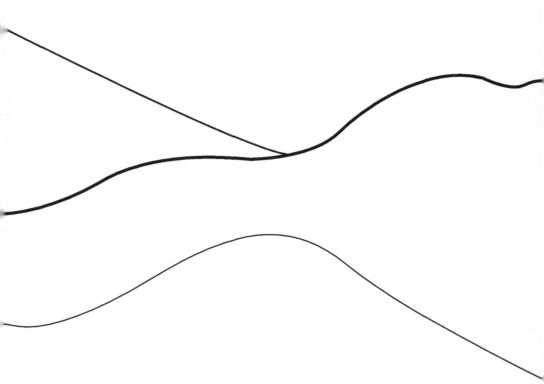

Back in the lounge they called the Big Room someone had lit a fire. I liked the Big Room. Its focal point was a large white-painted adobe fireplace with a softly curved facade, flanked by comfortable sofas and dark-leather armchairs around a coffee table. Near the fireplace, a barley-twist column supported the roof. The ceiling of wooden beams with slender peeled branches laid crosswise between them in a diagonal pattern made me think of an ocean swell.

The o-m and I were quietly relaxing when a crowd came in for a talk about Mabel. We listened in. The presenter knew just which aspects of Mabel's life would interest her guests. Her four marriages, her happy relationship with a Native American who became her fourth husband, her overweening ego, her success in surrounding herself with artists and writers, among them the great English novelist D H Lawrence. Mabel Ganson Evans Dodge Sterne Luhan, wealthy patron of the arts, who collected a new surname with each marriage, had summoned him to her colony, hoping he would write about Native Americans and also about her.

It felt odd trying to connect with Lawrence after so many years of hardly thinking about him. I wasn't sure I would still love the novels. Had no desire to reread *Women in Love* or *The Rainbow*. It would be scary to reread *Sons and Lovers* or *Lady Chatterley's Lover* because I had loved them so much. I hadn't read his writings based on Mabel or the spiritual quest stuff, *The Plumed Serpent* and short stories wheeling around the Native American psyche. Mabel repelled me slightly and Lawrence was so liable to rant.

Still, it was something to have seen his handiwork in the bathroom and to have read at the hotel about his relationship with Mabel and realise that New Mexico had given him important experiences: exploring Native American culture, coping with Mabel and his ever-worsening health. It was important to me that he was English, because I was brought up in England and in many ways I still thought 'Englishly'. Lawrence was a fellow countryman reassuring me, It's okay, don't be frightened. I've been here too.

We couldn't hang around the Mabel pilgrims any longer without being outed, so the o-m went back to our room and I went up a few steps into the east wing of the Big Room where three Americans were quietly relaxing. At first I looked around the alcove, which had another large fireplace, this time with an internal chimney that disappeared into the ceiling. Again, the ceiling was traditional adobe architecture, but much nearer to the floor, which gave the room a dark and slightly oppressive feel. There were photographs of a youngish Mabel and an imposing Tony in ceremonial dress.

The Americans were talking and after a while I joined in the conversation. Sam was a psychiatrist. His wife, Rebecca, I can't remember what she did or whether I was even told. They had known Sharon for thirty years but were now separated by diverging lives and the distance between New

Hampshire and Rhode Island, so the visit to Taos was an excuse for a reunion. They were disappointed in the hotel. It lacked modern conveniences such as internet in the guest rooms, but the other hotels were full.

Rebecca was suffering because her allergies had suddenly fired up again and she really thought the hotel management should have warned her there were cats. They planned, like me, to visit Taos Pueblo the next day and were dismayed to hear of my intention to walk there. Come with us, they offered. I went and asked the o-m if he wanted to come but he had visited the pueblo some years earlier and was in need of a restful day so I arranged to meet my new friends in the Big Room at 9 next morning. Meanwhile there was dinner at Lamberts.

Dinner at Lamberts was the last meal of that kind we would be able to afford, but the French menu was exquisitely prepared and presented. Next to our table two slim, elegant young women sat down to tuck away every available course with seamless ease. From their accents a little judicious eavesdropping told us one was French Canadian and the other French Arabian. When they finished eating the French Canadian approached us and the kindness of strangers came back into play, 'Do you like a lift back to the hotel? We are guests there too. Carol asked us to offer you a lift back.' Carol was the concierge at the Big House.

Next morning my new American amigos and I drove out to Taos Pueblo. We bought tickets and were given brochures which informed us the village was the oldest continuously inhabited community in the US. The sky was a clear blue, a perfect tonal match with the terracotta-coloured walls of the dwellings which rose in tiers with Taos Mountain forming their backdrop. Somewhere high above us among the Sangre de Cristo Mountains was the Blue Lake, which our brochure warned us was a sacred site, strictly off-limits to non-tribal members.

The buildings struck me as incomprehensibly strange. How could they have endured through centuries, how could *they* be part of America — the America in my mind that found its definition in weapons and wealth, racist violence and naked displays of power? The sun was casting such deep shadows that it was difficult to see things in their entirety. One part of the building would shadow another in such a way that it seemed to become a new entity.

Sam, Rebecca, Sharon and I tried to tally the various buildings with information in our brochures about their antiquity and the history of conflict first with the conquistadors and subsequently with settlers and US Homeland Security. I told the others what little I knew and they said I knew more than they who were home-grown Americans. In reality I was floundering. I wanted to understand but couldn't.

A young woman approached us. She told us she guided during study vacations because she wanted to give something back to her people. Summer walked us around the various structures, the church, the cemetery, the housing, most of it over 1000 years old. Here, surely, was Mabel's inspiration for the Big House. The adobe walls had survived the centuries through the assiduous application of fresh mud every year and were often a metre thick. Mabel had wanted simplicity and had fallen in love with adobe. 'Mud was mud, yes,' she wrote in *Edge of Taos Desert*, 'but mud was earth, something living and precious to be handled with understanding and care . . . The wonder of creation is in it, the wonder of transformation.'

In spite of the distorting sun, I could see cylindrical wooden shapes poking out of walls and was pleased to learn that they were the outer emanation of the beams or vigas that supported the ceilings, just as in Mabel's Big Room. Having seen Mabel's ceiling, I was able to imagine the viga and latilla construction inside the pueblo homes. I loved the fact that the inside connected with the outside in this way. Where doors were painted, their turquoise tones echoed the sky.

Doors, apparently, are a recent thing. In times gone by, people could get into their houses only by means of a ladder propped against the wall leading to an opening in the roof. At the scent of danger, the ladder could be pulled up like a portcullis. Now that conquistadors are less of a problem, doors are okay. Electricity and running water, however, are not. That's because the area was declared a World Heritage site by UNESCO in 1992. It was designated the 'First Living World Heritage' and power and running water would invalidate the classification. Instead, the Red Willow Creek that runs between the ancient north and south structures of the pueblo provides the only source of water, which has to be brought home in pots or water pails. Consequently, most of the pueblo inhabitants, about 2000 of them, live just outside the site proper, where they do have power and water. They only use the pueblo for ceremonial occasions. On the day I visited it felt empty, though about 150 people live in it year-round.

Outside the homes were beehive-shaped adobe ovens or horno, and, a few metres away, drying racks for jerky, corn, pumpkin, squash and bean crops, wild berries and animal hides for clothing. Summer explained these things but I couldn't get a sense of human beings living there. I couldn't get a sense of their consciousness. Summer told us some of the history connected with the pueblo, but I wasn't ready for it. I needed to find a way of relating to modern-day Pueblo life before I could slot the history into my brain. When Summer told us that all the Indians had been forced to take Spanish names, I could relate that to people living now, but names of unfamiliar historical figures and a succession of dates outlining aggressive actions and reactions between conquistador and Pueblo meant too little for my brain to retain them.

I did pick up that the first Europeans to see the Pueblo Indians were soldiers sent by a conquistador to explore the area in 1540 and that the chapel in front of us was built around 1619 by Spanish priests using forced Indian labour. The Indians were put under intense pressure to convert to Catholicism, which led to a bloody Pueblo attack on some Spanish settlements. Later on the Spanish engaged in a reconquest. Over the centuries, the Pueblo Indians took on some Catholic beliefs and practices while retaining a fierce ownership of their own customs and beliefs. Inside the chapel, the Virgin Mary is worshipped, not only as the mother of Jesus but also as mother nature. Her drapes change according to the seasons — white for winter, blue for spring, pink for summer, orange for autumn.

After Summer finished her tour, we wandered around alone, keeping a respectful distance from buildings in case they were occupied. Some of them had signs declaring them to be shops, welcoming visitors to come and look, but Sharon, fearing she would end up buying something, moved us on. I would have bought something just for the chance to talk except that I had no idea how to. How would a Native American feel about me as a white person? What could I say that didn't sound patronising? What right had I to be there at all? The last time I had any kind of consciousness about Native Americans was playing cowboys and Indians in the fields behind our house in Surrey. Imitation Stetson on my head, holster and gun on my undeveloped hips. Or feathers in my hair, bow and arrow in my hand. Indians were romantic, tall, strong, dignified, terrifying, incomprehensible. They broke the law, they had to be stopped, because cowboys were 'the good guys'.

Now that I'm home I realise why it was all so difficult. It's their *consciousness* I am interested in. I want to understand their consciousness, and at the time of visiting the pueblo I had no understanding at all, only a propensity to revere.

We wandered down to the river, across to the south side. As we looked beyond the pueblo to the Sangre de Cristo Mountains, Sam told me that these lands sacred to the Pueblo had been requisitioned in 1906 to be part of the national forest wilderness, but the tribe never gave up fighting for their return. Eventually in 1970, with the active support of President Nixon, Congress ordered 19,400 hectares of mountain lands including the Blue Lake to be returned to the Pueblo. But, I thought, Nixon was a bad guy!

I was expecting to go back to the hotel after this but struck lucky again when Sam invited me to come with them to the Millicent Rogers Museum. Millicent turned out to have been an arts patron to rival Mabel – and a glamour puss to outshine her. She arrived in Taos in 1947 after a break-up with Clark Gable and became a good friend of Mabel's husband Tony. Over subsequent years she built up a magnificent collection of Native American art and craft for display in the adobe house she renovated. Her penetrating eye for beauty enabled her to buy traditional Pueblo and Navajo art of enduring value. At the museum I saw thousands of pieces of Navajo and Pueblo jewellery, Navajo fabrics, Pueblo pottery and Apache basketry that she had collected. I began to feel curious about the woman behind all this, but the visit was over in what seemed like an instant. Sam took a photo of me with Rebecca and Sharon outside the museum and we moved on to the Rio Grande Gorge Bridge. Sam got vertigo.

Now I realise how little the river meant to me compared with the possibilities. I was just a tourist standing on a bridge looking down to a river below. A hundred and eighty metres below. All around was wild, stony desert and mountains. There wasn't much water in it. I was just a tourist being told that people have jumped off the bridge, that movies have used it as a backdrop. *Natural Born Killers*, for instance. And *Terminator Salvation*. Beside me Sam was trembling, his body radiating silence.

I had no sense of how the river connected with the land of the Southwest. That it begins in Colorado, dissects New Mexico in two and carries on down to the Gulf of Mexico, a journey of 3000 kilometres. Nor did I know that ever since 1848 when Mexico ceded a large tract of territory to the States, the middle of the Rio Grande has been the boundary marker between Mexico and the US. New cut-offs and islands caused by its spontaneous meanders have to be transferred back and forth between the two nations. So I did not realise that the Rio Grande I saw in Taos connected me to the thousands of asylum seekers who line its banks in Mexico, waiting interminably in wretched conditions and in constant fear of attack.

Lawrence remembered the river long after he returned to Europe. He recalled a dangerous light that rose over the mountains and touched 'the desert far-off, far-off, beyond the Rio Grande'. To me it was just a gorge that could give a man vertigo.

When Sam recovered, he drove us back to Taos and dropped me off at the hotel, where I visited the little bookstore at reception and got talking to Judy Gentry about the pueblo. She said she felt very at home there. For many years she was close to an inhabitant who was like a grandmother to her. Together they would sit out on the roof of her house and Judy would hear her stories, while down below someone used to pace like a town crier, telling everybody the pueblo news. Judy said the people's spiritual dances were the same now as thousands of years ago and their Tiwa language had remained unwritten because they wished it so.

I had a good look at the books for sale. It was from Judy I learned that Eusabio in Cather's novel *Death Comes for the Archbishop* was based on Tony. I remembered Eusabio, he was gentle and wise, of Navajo rather than Pueblo descent. Judy explained that adventurous women like Willa Cather, Mabel and Millicent Rogers loved Tony for the way he nurtured them, 'He encouraged them in their efforts to fulfil their potential.'

Such connections interested me so I bought a copy of *the Archbishop* and asked Judy to sign it. She wrote 'many blessings' on the flyleaf, a phrase I liked even more when Judy told me it was used by Native Americans as a wish for the good of the world, 'They pray to keep the sun coming up in the morning for all of us.'

The o-m and I walked down to the town for dinner, a much cheaper place this time. We had just finished our seafood enchilada when Sam appeared and offered us a lift back to the hotel when they finished their meal. The o-m was embarrassed about taking up a table while not eating so he ordered a slice of cheesecake. It was a huge helping and piled so high with cream, I couldn't face sharing. The o-m was not one for leaving food on his plate, so he struggled through, while I hoped Sam and the others didn't mind their unexpected wait.

I was sure the o-m had been dying to talk politics ever since he met my new friends and by the time we got back to the Big House, he was ready to ask Sam his question. Of course it concerned the forthcoming general election — would Hillary win? As Sam paused, the o-m hazarded, 'It's in the bag, isn't it?' and Sam nodded, 'Yes', or words to that effect. At that time it did look to be in the bag. Bernie Sanders seemed too far outside the political arena to be taken seriously and Donald Trump was a joke. A joke that came back to haunt.

On our last morning it snowed. Outside, the world became quiet and the branches of trees hung down under layers of whiteness. We sat in the Big Room by the big fire watching the snow fall and wondering carelessly how difficult it was going to be to walk to the bus station with the suitcases. We had reached that state beloved of travellers where nothing is a worry, but Judy worried for us. When the o-m asked her where he could get a new battery for his hearing aid, she organised the maintenance man to go. She didn't want us walking in the snow, either for a hearing aid or to the bus station. I flushed inwardly again. We had become embarrassingly high maintenance for all these kind Americans.

The red berries of a bush outside the window stood out now against the white snow while the adobe buttresses were outlined with a thin snow-white pencil. It was eerie and beautiful and it made me not want to leave. There was a pushing against the great front door and into the lounge stepped a young woman. She deposited her suitcases in a corner and proceeded to the sofa nearest the fire. I began thinking up things to say beyond the brief hello we had already exchanged but the snow princess had a mission. Sheets of white paper on her lap, a pen in her hand, words began to flow. We were in the presence of Mabel's legacy, the drawing power of her historic community. Came Judy to announce that Mabel's room was 'ready' but the new guest continued writing. The Flow was with her.

The clock ticked on and the snow continued to fall. The snow princess put away her working tools and announced by a barely perceptible change in mien her readiness for conversation. We were dying to know what she was writing and now the snow princess was glad to oblige. She was writing a novel in which Mabel would appear as a ghost. I realised then that Mabel would never die.

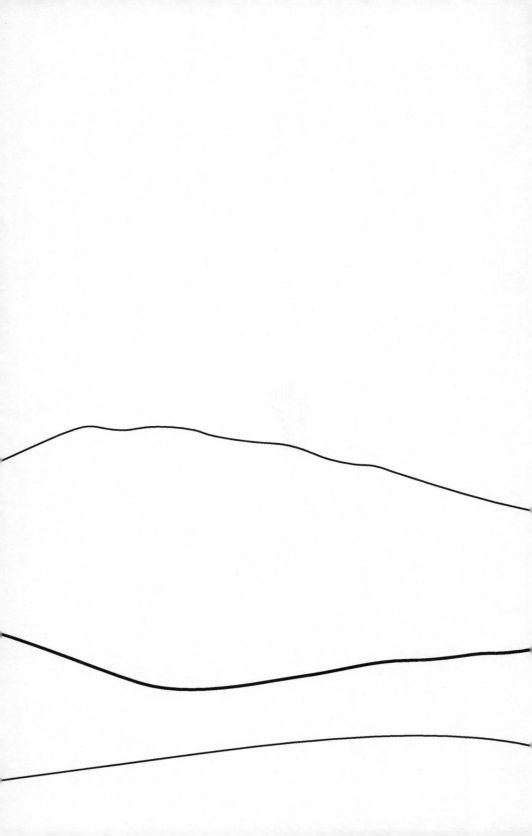

4
Lawrence and Mabel in Terra Incognita

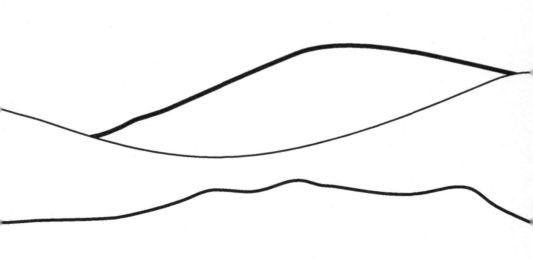

I had come home and it was time for roulette. My journey had raised many questions. I wanted answers. I knew Taos was a place artists and writers came to for escape, but I didn't understand why. I made assumptions. That Lawrence was looking for ways to stay away from England and went to Taos to write. That Mabel had gone to New Mexico much as I had — out of curiosity, without any particular thing driving her. I knew the Pueblo Indians had a long history and that it involved conquistadors, Catholic priests and the Manifest Destiny of the United States, but I didn't know what that history was. I didn't know anything about Pueblo culture and beliefs. I didn't know how Mabel had managed to bring so many illustrious people to her home nor what was in it for them. I didn't even know what the territory of New Mexico was like, beyond the narrow strip of land from Santa Fe to Taos and back. But I understood that the writers and artists who had inhabited the building I had just stayed in had gone on to create works of art that could well cast illumination on all these mysteries.

The Big House would provide a grounding point of reference. The Big House was something I had *experienced*. It was the litmus paper that changed my consciousness of America from blue to pink, and the books on sale at reception were my first resource. In addition to Cather's novel I bought *Literary Pilgrims* by Lynn Cline and noted many more titles I might want to follow up. Judy brought my attention to Frank Waters, who had written eloquently and incisively about Native American peoples. I saw that Lois Palken Rudnick had written books on Mabel and the utopian nature of her vision.

Roulette would guide the writing of the book. My board would display everything that had impinged on me during my visit and the dice would naturally alight where the strength of impact was greatest.

My first roll of the dice alighted on Lawrence, whose presence at the Big House now impregnated my own house. I had felt it in the windows of Mabel's bathroom and I felt it now in our unfinished business. I had responded to his lyricism and explicit descriptions of sex as a schoolgirl in rebellion against parents and church. Dancing with his ghost would offer a kind of exorcism, not because I wanted to extinguish his influence on my life, but because I wanted to experience him as a grown-up.

From reading *Kangaroo* I had some knowledge of Lawrence as a traveller, but none of what drove him to the New World. Apparently it had much to do with World War I. He did not share the common belief that it had achieved something worth having, let alone that it was the war to end all wars. While political leaders driven by idealists set about creating a League of Nations, hoping to bring Europe together in such a way that war would never again present itself as an option, Lawrence sorrowed at the effects on his fellow human beings. How much hard-won enlightenment had been lost and how insidiously mechanisation was destroying their souls.

Desperate for somewhere in the world that cherished human dignity and psychic health, he put his faith in America, and in Native Americans in particular, 'I must see America. I believe one can feel hope there. I think that there the life comes up from the roots, crude but vital. Here, the whole tree of life is dying.'[3]

His poem 'Terra Incognita', written just after the end of the war, is a cry from the heart.

> There are vast realms of consciousness still undreamed
> of, vast ranges of experience, like the humming of
>   unseen harps,
> we know nothing of, within us.
>
> Oh when man has escaped from the barbed-wire
>   entanglement
> of his own ideas and his own mechanical devices
> there is a marvellous rich world of contact and sheer
>   fluid beauty
> and fearless face-to-face awareness of now-naked life
> and me, and you, and other men and women
> and grapes, and ghouls, and ghosts and green moonlight
> and ruddy-orange limbs stirring the limbo
> of the unknown air, and eyes so soft,
> softer than the space between the stars,
> and all things, and nothing, and being and not-being
> alternately palpitant,
> when at last we escape the barbed-wire enclosure
> of *Know Thyself*, knowing we can never know,
> we can but touch, and wonder, and ponder, and make
>   our effort
> and dangle in a last fastidious fine delight

as the fuchsia does, dangling her reckless drop
of purple after so much putting forth
and slow mounting marvel of a little tree.

In his search for 'fearless face-to-face awareness of now' Lawrence turned his gaze towards America years before his physical journey into its interior. He had begun seeking out its classic literature at a time when few in Britain or indeed in America thought there was such a thing. His efforts, later published as *New Poems* and *Studies in Classic American Literature*, helped him begin to understand people whose 'spirit of place' was very different from his own. The idea of 'dark races' fascinated him. He wanted to prove he could step outside his own cultural boundaries and see from their point of view.

Already the dice are rolling again and this time they settle on Mabel who, since she was the one to call Lawrence to America, must be brought into play right now. As a young woman she too had been entranced by his writing. How exactly his dream of the integrated body and spirit meshed with hers! The author of *Sons and Lovers*, *The Rainbow* and *Women in Love* incarnated the 'eternal feminine' and understood, just as she did, that Western civilisation was bringing on its own destruction.[4] Mabel's vision for her artist's colony in Taos entailed nothing less than the transformation of America. For her, Lawrence was the only person with the potential to see truly the terra incognita that was the land of Native Americans, the only writer who could make it real and alive to others.

Mabel's upbringing in a wealthy banking family with strict Victorian attitudes towards sex and success had saddled her with an insatiable need to be loved. Failing that, to be the centre of attention. Despite sparing no effort to be 'joyful, certain, strong', she suffered repeatedly from depression. Lovers, marriages, Freudian psychoanalysis, liberal causes, modern art, she tried them all. And in trying them she made a surprising discovery — her genius for bringing together reformers and artists of all kinds. Upon her second marriage, she and Edwin Dodge moved to Italy where Mabel converted a former Medici palace near Florence to a new Renaissance-like salon. People such as Gertrude and Leo Stein, Alice B Toklas, André Gide, James Joyce, Jacques-Émile Blanche, Pablo Picasso, Arthur Rubinstein and Bernard Berenson became her guests.

After her return to New York in 1912, she created a new salon in Washington Square in avant-garde Greenwich Village. As war drew near in Europe, and New York sagged under the weight of its love affair with material wealth, many of the patrons of her famous 'Wednesday Evenings' were searching for a new kind of consciousness, but to Mabel's way of thinking they brought too much of the old world with them in a frenzy to escape themselves. Yes they would create new art forms, yes they would remake the world, but they had no time to simply 'be', to know their inner selves. And never the time to be kind.

The second marriage foundered and a third was undertaken, but despite her new start, huge wealth, enormous energy, Freudian psychoanalysis and the outstanding success of her New York salon, Mabel was little closer to finding inner peace. She banished her third husband, artist Maurice Sterne, to New Mexico after he flirted with another woman, but it was he who came up with a mission that would change her life. 'Dearest girl,' he wrote from Santa Fe. 'Do you want an object in life? Save the Indians, their art — culture — reveal it to the world!'[5]

Save the Indians! When I read this, I feared for Mabel. As the o-m has pointed out, I have something of the spirit of missionary zeal myself and it has sometimes led me to overlook the essence in human interaction that makes it authentic. According to the o-m, do-gooders do the most harm of all and he may have a point. Would Mabel be an exception? She had company. In her desire to improve the world, she was squarely within an American tradition. She had wealth, a sense of entitlement, she suffered, she saw herself as a significant and compassionate player. A purpose in life could be the solution to her problems. Putting to one side her jealousy and anger with Maurice, Mabel packed her bags.

At the time of her arrival in New Mexico in 1917, it had been an American state for only five years. The story of how the Native Americans were deprived of their lands and domains first by Spaniards, then by Mexicans, then by Texans and finally by the United States was one of greed and racial intolerance. It was a wild country, full of untamed geological forms holding out the promise of gold, and of people whose ways could appear barbaric to those whose barbarism had a different hue.

During the nineteenth century, Santa Fe developed into a trading hub between the United States, central Mexico and Mexican California. In 1879 the railway came to New Mexico and, as happens with railways, the region it dissected changed forever. At first the railroad company highlighted New Mexico's elevation and dry atmosphere as a magnet for people suffering from tuberculosis and other lung ailments, but towards the end of the century it found another marketing tool, using images of Native Americans in its guidebooks. In an innovative form of patronage for the arts, it offered painters free travel passes, displaying in its waiting rooms and restaurants their renditions of the region as a beautiful and exotic place to visit. Many of the artists moved to New Mexico.

A further source of tourism evolved as tourists flocked to visit the painters at work in their studios. Native American ceremony and ritual began to feature more and more prominently in their work. Taos, home to one of the oldest continuously inhabited pueblos in the United States, was especially popular. Indian culture underwent commodification while contemporary American culture exploded in new directions. Native Americans looked on uneasily.

Mabel had never seen such landscapes. Stark tablelands or mesas rose out of the desert, with nothing around except arid soil and sparse vegetation. Here was no landscape at the mercy of human intervention, here were fundamental forces of nature. Wind, sun and rain playing ducks and drakes with rock. As Mabel wrote in *Taos and Its Artists*, here were 'beauty and terror, sun and shadow'. And here were human societies living in close harmony with those forces, often on the top of the mesa. She wanted this new world of 'golden light' and 'abysmal shadows' to be itself alone, unconnected with any past she had ever known. Here she was witnessing the origins of life and here she would be able to begin again.

She lost no time in making contact with the people of Taos Pueblo. There she met Tony Lujan, a Pueblo American who seemed to exemplify in one human being everything she was looking for in her new world. He was married and so, at the beginning, was she, but the relationship quickly developed into something that genuinely touched the core of Mabel's being. On a practical level, she initiated divorce proceedings with Sterne and made her new relationship viable by agreeing, at Mary Austin's insistence, to pay $35 a month to Tony's wife as long as she didn't make trouble. A move that didn't go down well with the pueblo.

Tony was gentle and accepting. He did not idealise her, in fact he often barely spoke, but Mabel decided that the talk, talk, talk of New York served for little except to diminish one's spiritual energy. She often found herself speechless in Tony's presence but it didn't matter. Talking was not the only way to communicate, not even the most significant. The old ways of responding belonged to a different world. Mabel began to see that her old world emphasised the individual at the expense of belonging. In her memoir *Edge of Taos Desert* she wrote,

> Not a day passed that Tony did not make me realize how rough and insensitive I was, and that all my past sensitiveness had been employed in self-feeling and never in fellow-feeling. When he saw I suffered from this dawning awareness of myself as an isolated egotist, he consoled me.[6]

The music she heard at the pueblo helped her understand that communal music expressed more than the voices of individuals. 'It is easy to believe that a tribe composes the body of some vast Being, and that its health and strength must depend upon unison in the tribe.'[7]

In her memoir she reflected that divisions and subdivisions of the world had guided the activities of everyone she had known. Fragmenting the world into parts and the parts into ever tinier fractions had supercharged the reach of technology, enabling people to live in greater physical comfort but at the price of cluttering the world with devices. Eventually the individual human being, 'elaborate, unhappy, modern man', had become cut off from his source. This was very similar to Lawrence's evolving view.

When I visited the Big House, Mabel meant little to me. I glimpsed the spirit of the house but failed to see the woman behind the flamboyant life. Back home I slowly began to fold back the layers of her complex personality and found an unexpectedly interesting and sympathetic character. A hundred years after Mabel, I too was concerned with what the 'raging lust for individuality and separateness' had done to a communal way of experiencing. Although I had alighted on Mabel by accident, she was enriching my understanding of America and offering me an avenue to connection.

The house that Tony and Mabel built together in Taos was in total contrast to her previous homes. Not only because of the building material, which was adobe, or because of the architecture, which was Pueblo, but on account of the spirit in which it was built. Everywhere she had lived before, she had sensed alienation between the labourers and those they built for.

> Houses being torn down, streets being torn up, new buildings arising upon old sites, and everywhere this activity was taken for granted by most people as a miserable necessity that had to be accepted along with the antagonistic, cut-off feeling in the men engaged in it; the unfriendliness and the sullenness of workmen was an element in everyday life everywhere encountered and everywhere sidestepped . . . But here in Taos it was delightful to be with these workmen, for there was no indignity in raising a house, and nothing sordid in either the materials or in their use of them.[8]

As her workmen transformed mud into adobe, the house grew out of the land itself, enabling the entire natural world to be her home. She was filled with hope and idealism. Here in Taos she would gather artists, writers, photographers. They would rediscover an original relationship with the universe, unmediated by the texts and art forms of earlier ages and other places. Instead of developing an art focussed on alienation they would celebrate organic connection between individual and community. And to bring that mysterious connection to life, the writer she needed was Lawrence. In December 1920 the Big House was finished and a year later, inspired by Lawrence's writings on Sardinia,[9] Mabel issued an invitation. She wrote that in Taos she had found a place that echoed the dawn of the world.

When Lawrence received Mabel's letter, he was already embarked on a journey through India, Ceylon and Australia en route to America. He needed to experience a shift of consciousness, as may happen when one is faced with two different ways of being in the world, and believed he would find it through the intersection between 'Red' and 'White' America:

> Americans must take up life where the Red Indian, the Aztec, the Maya, the Incas left it off . . . They must catch the pulse of life which Cortes and Columbus murdered. There lies the real continuity; not between Europe and the new States, but between the murdered Red America and the seething White America.[10]

Lawrence and Frieda arrived in Taos in September 1922. Mabel welcomed them to her home and, as she had hoped, Lawrence agreed to collaborate on a proposed book about her experience as a wealthy patroness from New York coming to live in the Southwest. However, Frieda, who had given up a husband and her children to be with Lawrence, was not someone to be left out of an equation. Both she and Mabel deeply admired the great writer in their midst, but while Mabel swelled with the importance of her mission in life, Frieda saw only the desire of a rival to use her husband for her own purposes.

Lawrence dithered, then concluded Frieda was right — and Mabel herself would acknowledge in *Lorenzo in Taos* that she had wanted to seduce his spirit so that she could make him carry out certain things. Her purpose required nothing less than 'his soul, his will, his creative imagination, and his lighted vision'.[11]

Well, I can hear Lawrence saying, she's not having it! He was not a person to hand over either his soul or his will to another person, especially not a woman. In how many

and : why adore him?

novels had he not described the ever-present danger of being dominated by another's will and of losing one's own? The threat, for Lawrence, was existential, because in many ways he *wanted* to surrender his will. Thus, his fascination with what he saw as the Native American way of seeing the world. Again and again he explored his personal conflict in his writing. It's there in *The Plumed Serpent*, the novel he began writing soon after his arrival in New Mexico and which draws on Mabel for its English heroine, Kate Leslie. Kate feels a sense of alienation from her own cultural heritage and is drawn to the more elemental one she encounters in Mexico. She falls into agonising indecision, however, when faced with permanently abandoning her culture's emphasis on individual freedom. She does eventually surrender her individuality to a different kind of consciousness, but at huge personal cost,

> It meant a submission she had never made. It meant
> the death of her individual self. It meant abandoning
> so much, even her own very foundations. For she had
> believed truly that every man and every woman alike was
> founded on the individual.
> Now, must she admit that the individual was an illusion
> and a falsification? There was no such animal. Except
> in the mechanical world. In the world of machines, the
> individual machine is effectual. The individual, like
> the perfect being, does not and cannot exist in the vivid
> world. We are all fragments. And at the best, halves.[12]

After a couple of months living at the Big House, Lawrence could not stand Mabel's domination any longer, so he and Frieda moved twenty-seven kilometres away to a cabin on a ranch, where they stayed for a few months before leaving for a year in Mexico. On their return to the Big House, his relationship with Mabel began sweetly but soured within a couple of months. Mabel offered Lawrence a sixty-four hectare ranch she had originally bought for her son. He declined, hating the idea of being beholden to her, but Frieda accepted on his behalf. In acknowledgement of the gift, Lawrence gave her the manuscript of *Sons and Lovers*.

Kiowa Ranch might be the perfect solution but there was plenty of work to do to make it habitable. Brett's first impression was of horror. One house had been a cowshed for years, she thought. The second house could be made fit to live in, if properly cleaned. The third house was sunny but might be too small to fit in a bed. She need not have worried. Lawrence, an enthusiastic DIY man, set to work with her, scrubbing first and then putting in new props, making new foundations, digging trenches, chopping wood, building a porch. Lawrence tackled the filthy, sweaty work of cleaning rat dirt and nests out of the attic. Frieda did the cooking. Mabel came often, bringing Indians, taking them away, bringing pots and pans and stores. At first she slept with Pueblo in Tony's tepee up on the hill. When it was ready, she took over the second house for her frequent visits.

The household was not always peaceful. As a chronicler, Brett was handicapped by her deafness. Often I was frustrated by her autobiography when a drama was unfolding between Frieda and Lawrence, sometimes involving Mabel too, and Brett, my informer, was unable to understand what was happening. She was usually an apparently innocent bystander, but it seems that both Frieda and Mabel were jealous of her place in Lawrence's heart. Lawrence was often exasperated with Frieda, who frequently engaged in a battle of wills with him.

As for Mabel, he described her in a letter to Frieda's mother as 'a cooing raven of ill-omen, a little buffalo' and once even told a friend he wanted to murder her, yet unwittingly she did him great service. As a physical embodiment of New

Woman in search of spiritual and emotional redemption, she provided a basis for characters through which to explore his own conflicted relationship with Native Americans.

In 1924 he wrote three stories set at least partly in New Mexico. In 'The Woman Who Rode Away', Mabel's unnamed incarnation is ritually, though not unwillingly, sacrificed by an Indian tribe (he did say he wanted to murder her).

'St Mawr', which at 130 pages is really a novella, is a work of astounding power and, to my mind, one of Lawrence's very best. He draws upon Mabel for one of the two main characters and her character leaps off the page, often to great comedic effect. Although a character 'based on' is not the same as biography, the character rings true for Mabel, making it satisfying to conflate the two.

The story presents several characters who live in a kind of exile. Mrs Witt and her daughter Lou are Americans living in London. Mrs Witt's groom, Phoenix, is a Navajo American, while Lou's groom Lewis is an unkempt Welshman with long hair. Neither Phoenix nor Lewis wants to be in service but they have no choice.

Lou is married to an unlikely kind of Australian, Rico, son of a baronet who is 'being an artist'. She is filled with doubt and uncertainty — about her marriage, about who she is, what she wants, and what is real and has meaning. Just as she is finding Rico increasingly unsatisfactory, enter St Mawr, a magnificent but unpredictable stallion and at the same time an embodiment of the male energy and power that Lou finds so lacking in Rico. Lou must own him; she decrees that Rico must ride him. Rico does and is injured. While he is away convalescing Lou becomes fascinated by Phoenix, the Navajo groom, a man of few words and much mystery, while her mother is mesmerised by the Welsh groom whom Lou acquired along with St Mawr. Both represent a kind of manhood the women yearn for and both resent having to work for the women and be their inferiors.

Mrs Witt is Lawrence's chosen vehicle for Mabel's energy, certainty and dominance. Before long she intimidates Lewis into letting her cut his hair, much as Mabel surely might have done.

> Mrs Witt, happily on the war path, was herself again. She didn't care for work, actual work. But she loved trimming. She loved arranging unnatural and pretty salads, devising new and piquant-looking ice-creams, having a turkey stuffed exactly as she knew a stuffed turkey in Louisiana, with chestnuts and butter and stuff, or showing a servant how to turn waffles on a waffle-iron, or to bake a ham with brown sugar and cloves and a moistening of rum. She liked pruning rose-trees, or beginning to cut a yew hedge into shape.[13]

After the accident Rico's friends demand the stallion be shot but Mrs Witt takes the side of St Mawr, implying her son-in-law may have been to blame. She had told Lou she'd love to pour a cup of tea into Mrs Vyner's hat and her defence of St Mawr brings her comparable satisfaction.

> She looked from one to the other with a faint and gracious little bow, her black eyebrows arching in her eighteenth-century face like black rainbows, and her full, bold grey eyes absolutely incomprehensible.[14]

I am reminded of Mabel in Mrs Witt's energy, restlessness and need for a particular mysterious kind of dynamism that could flourish between her and a man. She dissects her own nature in a manner reminiscent of one of Mabel's memoirs.

> She had long ago decided that her nature was a destructive force. But then, she justified herself, she had only destroyed that which was destructible. If she could have

found something indestructible, especially in men, though she would have fought against it, she would have been glad at last to be defeated by it.[15]

The story advances when mother and daughter decide to return to America, to set up a life on a ranch in the Southwest. Lou's relinquishing of old alliances of friendship, marriage and life with the smart set in London sets her free. In Texas, she and Mrs Witt leave Lewis and St Mawr himself in Texas and journey to Santa Fe. Dissatisfied with the town and the 'mayonnaise intimacy' of the hotel dining room, Lou and Phoenix drive off to investigate a small ranch that has come on the market.

The denouement of Lou's liberation from crippling uncertainty is conveyed through Lawrence's powerful depiction of life on the ranch as it was for previous owners. 'St Mawr' vindicates my adolescent love of Lawrence's work. I find the prose unutterably beautiful, while a sense of mystery compels me to turn the pages. His vignettes are funny and succinct. He gives full rein to an astonishing creative power that comes from a place way beyond intellect, while he grapples with things that fascinate, disturb and oppress him — the mystery he finds in exotic cultures and peoples, the corrosive nature of class systems and racism, his search for the kind of masculinity he finds missing in his post-war world.

Lawrence wrote 'The Woman Who Rode Away', 'St Mawr' and 'The Princess' at Kiowa and Brett typed them up for him. Brett herself features as the main character, Dollie Urquhart, in 'The Princess', a story about two people suffering an overwhelming sense of exile, Dollie from her father's obsessive claim of royal family blood which set her apart, and Domingo Romero from his noble Spanish lineage which had degenerated into 'Mexican peasants'. Romero is based on a married Native American who worked on the ranch and with whom Lawrence discovered Brett was having an affair. The characters' inability to find a comfortable home for their psyches leads to death and madness. Lawrence wrote that the intense feeling of sadness in his three New Mexican stories was true to the reality of the country.[16]

Somehow the bond between Lawrence and Mabel endured. Up to a point they were looking for the same thing. Both were keenly aware of the damage that materialism had done to people's spiritual health and they wanted to find another path: for Mabel, one which could offer a true American identity; for Lawrence, one that offered a way forward from the destructiveness of Europe. Both were fascinated by the pueblo and wanted to see it without Western blinkers. In his 1927 book of essays, *Mornings in Mexico*, Lawrence put it with style,

> The Indian is not in line with us. He's not coming our way. His whole being is going a different way from ours. And the minute you set eyes on him you know it.

He warned against trying to express one stream of consciousness in terms of another. 'The only thing you can do is to have a little Ghost inside you which sees both ways, or even many ways.'

The little ghost was Taos' gift to Lawrence.

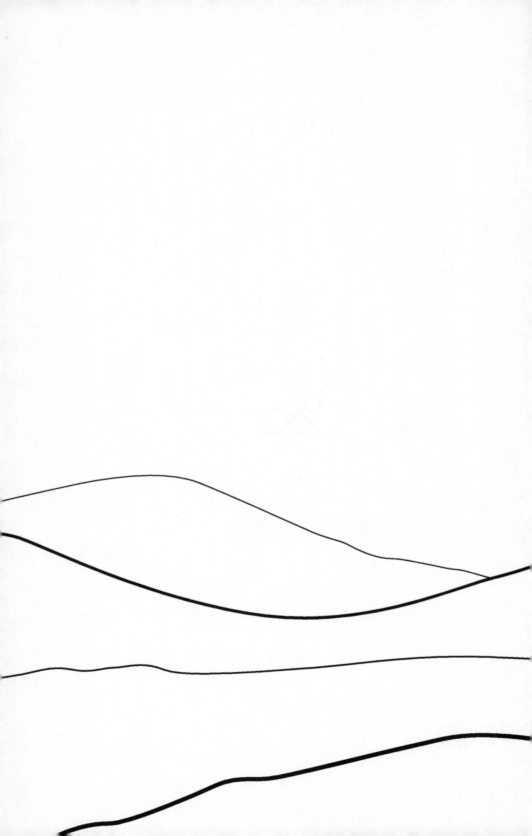

5
Saving
the Indians

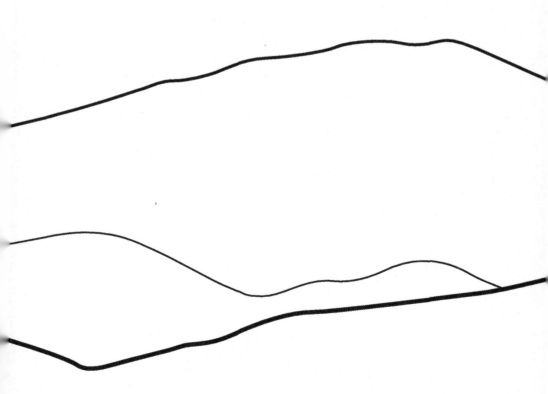

When Mabel started visiting the Taos Pueblo, she saw evidence of serious diseases such as TB, dysentery and trachoma. Doctors earned less on the reservations and were in short supply. In fact, for all ten pueblos north of Santa Fe, there were only two doctors and even supplies were short. Nice work for a saviour at large. Mabel worked out what medical supplies were needed for the population she estimated at 600 and began supplying them to the medic who worked with the Taos Pueblo.

Three years in, she persuaded a sociologist friend from her salon days, John Collier, to join her in Taos. Like Mabel he was dismayed by the sorry state of cooperative and communal values since the advent of mechanisation. Like her, he believed in the potential for Native American cultural values to help restore them. As America moved closer to entering World War I, he witnessed growing hysteria against workers, radicals and immigrants. Then, as the war dragged on, he saw how a herd mentality could incapacitate the forces that normally kept paranoia and repression in check. By the time he received Mabel's letter of invitation in 1919 he was keen to engage with a totally different kind of culture.

In Taos, Mabel and Tony had been busy adding guest houses to the Big House and Collier and his family were able to take up residence as the first occupants of the Two-Story House. For two years Collier studied the history and current life of Native Americans. He began to suspect that syphilis existed at the pueblo and mentioned this to Mabel.

She could not have been more appalled. As she finally acknowledged in one of her unpublished memoirs, 'The Statue of Liberty', syphilis had doomed her second and third marriages. Her second husband, Edwin Dodge, was no longer infectious when they married and her third, Maurice Sterne, discovered it after they were married. Luckily for Mabel, he too was in the later stages of the disease, so she remained uninfected, but the disease made both husbands physically repulsive to her. Just as bad, the loneliness of keeping it a guilty secret, as everyone did in those days, meant that Maurice and Mabel felt they were totally alone in the world with it. It was not until 2000 that her biographer, Lois Palken Rudnick, would be able to see the memoirs for the first time.

Collier wanted to investigate his suspicion of syphilis in the pueblo, so he suggested to Mabel that a physiologist should look into its incidence. But for Mabel, confirmation of the disease would undermine the pueblo as her Arcadian refuge. How could a people she saw as 'clean and wholesome and free of the sin and decadence of the world' contain that unspeakable disease?

Collier was not to be put off. He lost no time in introducing Dr Eshref Shevky and his wife Marion to Mabel and his instinct proved right because the Shevkys soon became treasured house guests. Tony took Shevky to the pueblo and Mabel offered to pay for Wassermann tests on all its men and women. It wasn't easy to persuade the people to give up their blood believing, as they did, that it might fall into the hands of witches. Many disapproved of Mabel's relationship with one of their married chiefs and were suspicious of her intentions, so Tony, who trusted Collier absolutely, took the test first. Results showed that around 12 per cent of Taos Pueblo, which was probably about 2000-strong at the time, had contracted the scourge. Tony, as Mabel expected, was declared free of it. Confirmation of her belief that her lover was 'beyond corruption'.

Meanwhile in Washington a new bill was being drafted. The Bursum Bill was no less than an assault on the Pueblo way of life which, if passed, would throw the Pueblos' very survival into doubt. A decade of rising intolerance of racial and ethnic minorities had created fertile ground for its passage. In principle, it was the age-old story of a land battle between the coloniser and the colonised. Specifically, the bill arose out of a long-standing property dispute between the Pueblos and their invaders. For the forty years preceding 1913, Pueblo lands had been available for purchase and squatting, allowing many Hispanos and Anglos to take up residence, but that year everything changed. From 1913 the Pueblos did not have the right to sell or give up their lands and by 1921 around 3000 Hispanos and Anglos were facing uncertainty about their rights on Pueblo land.

Armed conflict with Native Americans was looking increasingly likely and the Bursum Bill aimed to settle the matter. It would give clear title to any non-Pueblo residents who could prove they owned a title dating back to at least 1902 and thereby would settle matters favourably not only for settlers and ranchers but also for corporations with an interest in oil, coal and other minerals and for the State of New Mexico itself. Opponents of the bill estimated it would deprive Pueblos of at least 24,000 hectares, most of it valuable irrigated land.

The new bill was deliberately kept under wraps and John Collier learned of its existence following its third iteration in Congress, after it had been approved by the Senate. And the Pueblos had not been informed of the bill at all. However, the immensely popular and influential General Federation of Women's Clubs (GFWC), a women's volunteer service promoting unity in diversity, was already rallying to the Pueblo cause. Its leader, Stella Atwood, told Collier about it and appointed him the organisation's research agent. Collier, who took inspiration from recently witnessing the Deer Dance at the pueblo, wrote an essay to launch his crusade against the Bursum Bill and informed Mabel. The energy of missionary zeal on behalf of Native American rights began to flow through their veins.

It was September 1922, the same month that D H Lawrence arrived and became Collier's next-door neighbour. Although Lawrence was not a political activist by nature, he was persuaded by Mabel to write an article that was published in the *New York Times* and he also signed her Protest of Artists and Writers Against the Bursum Bill. This petition formed the basis of a nationwide campaign, the first in US history to appeal for Native American rights. Many artists and writers signed it, sharing a belief that the Pueblo way of life could become a way for all Americans of overcoming what was lacking in modern society. The embodiment of this in Native American and Anglo music, painting and poetry endowed the campaign with mass public appeal and helped defuse racial intolerance.

Many of the two million women who belonged to the GFWC wrote letters and sent telegrams to their Congressman arguing against the bill. The artists and activists formed lobbying groups and the conservative

Bureau of Catholic Indian Missions and the Eastern Association of Indian Affairs, well stocked with political savvy, also came on board. Together they fought claims that Pueblo religious dances and rituals were savage and obscene and should be regulated. They also stood with Native American parents for the right of their children to attend puberty rituals even when this required taking special leave from their government boarding schools.

Mabel was in her element. She not only believed utterly in the cause but was also perfectly positioned to help achieve its goals. Operating as Collier's publicity agent, she was able to secure serious attention in the most prestigious national journals and also in Congress. She put Collier in touch with other artists, writers and reformers, who took up the cause. Reluctant to publish articles in her own name, she nonetheless ensured that persuasive articles appeared.

Tony played an important liaison role. He brought Collier to the Pueblo villages to explain the destructive effect a successful bill would have on their way of life. The Pueblos came together to form the All Pueblo Council (APC), which quickly grew adept at lobbying. The council drafted 'An Appeal by the Indians of New Mexico to the people of the United States' which the GFWC distributed to politicians. It appealed to the American people's sense of justice and fair play.

> We, the Pueblo Indians, have always been self-
> supporting and have not been a burden on the
> government. We have lived in peace with our fellow-
> Americans even while we have watched the gradual
> taking away of our lands and waters . . . We have reached
> a point where we must either live or die . . . Now we
> discover that the Senate has passed a bill, called the
> Bursum bill, which will complete our destruction . . .
> We have studied the bill over and found that this bill

will deprive us of our happy life by taking away our lands and water and will destroy our pueblo government and customs . . . The bill will take away our self-respect and make us dependent on the Government . . .[17]

At Mabel's urging Mary Austin, who had made the Big House her HQ for research among the Pueblos, accompanied the delegates to Washington to testify to Congress. Everything was done with dignity and quiet insistence. In New York a group dancing to the music of drums reduced the Stock Exchange to silence. Public and congressional opinion began to turn against the bill.

Meanwhile, Mabel conceived a new world plan. It was very grand, setting out to save both the culture and agriculture of the Indians. She was convinced that Americans were now amenable to incorporating the best of Native American culture into their own lives. In a letter to Mary Austin, she speculated with trademark emphasis and reiteration that it might be possible for appreciation of Indian life and culture to become an integral part of the American psyche. Her plan could underpin a social experiment that would bring Americans spiritual peace, and she offered Collier her home as a centre from which all could be accomplished. Collier shared Mabel's vision, but cautioned that they would have to build a national movement and solid political clout if they were ever to achieve the things Mabel had in mind.

The bill was defeated in January 1923 to great rejoicing, but its proponents were fighters too. They put forward a compromise bill, which some of the Pueblos were inclined to accept. However, it offered no compensation for land and water rights and Collier believed that 75 per cent of the claims against the lands were not based on legal title. The bill could have fatally divided the parties who had opposed the first one, but Pueblo confidence in Collier was so great that the chiefs publicly rejected it, after which Collier masterminded a more genuine compromise. A lands board was created to ensure the status and boundaries of Pueblo lands were correctly established; non-Indian claimants had to show continuous possession from 1902; both Indians and settlers were to be compensated for lost lands and all money awarded to the Pueblos was to be tagged for the purchase of land and water rights.

Collier worried that Mabel's relationship with Tony could put it all at risk. The government's Bureau of Indian Affairs (BIA) was campaigning against the barbarism of Pueblo customs and dances and the immorality of its culture. As Tony was still married to his Pueblo wife, this provided fodder for the argument, and the press was not slow to bring it to everyone's attention. Collier and Mary Austin advised the pair to wed. Mabel and Tony were willing, trusting that this would defuse the controversy that swirled around them. They changed Tony's surname to Luhan for reasons of pronunciation and married in April 1923, but this only gave the press grounds for another field day. According to the *Pittsburgh Post*, 'Why Bohemia's Queen Married an Indian Chief', she had fallen into the muscular arms of her Indian chief to be smothered by his kisses. However, Mabel wasn't fazed and Collier's Pueblo Lands Board Act was passed in June 1924. Even now it's a source of inspiration for contemporary activists.

Collier went on to broaden his reach as a reformer, working on Indian-rights cases from Arizona, California and Montana. In time he became Commissioner of Indian Affairs. Reforms quickly followed, the most far-reaching of which was the Indian Reorganization Act of 1934. Overnight, government policy changed from forced assimilation to cultural pluralism. A spin-off was that young American Indians began to demonstrate political sophistication and a new assertiveness in working for Indian rights. Throughout the rest of his career in politics, Collier's reforms honoured the vision he and Mabel had created during the 1920s. His commitment never faltered.

Meanwhile, Mabel's ghosts returned to haunt her shortly after her marriage when she discovered she had contracted syphilis from Tony. After her previous near-brushes with the disease, it was a devastating development and a watershed in her relationship with the man she had believed beyond corruption. It seems likely that it ended their sexual relationship, though the companionship and sense of being twin souls endured. When she finally allowed herself in 1947 to write about the disaster, she was deeply depressed about her marriage and in particular the corrosive part played in it by syphilis, which she thought of as the wages of sin, 'all the time I was burning with the grief of my misfortune which I felt was undeserved and almost too much to bear. I felt set apart from other people and I was very lonely.' In her 2012 publication *The Suppressed Memoirs of Mabel Dodge Luhan*, Rudnick included many illuminating extracts from the memoir.

Lawrence was unaware of all this. Just before Mabel and Tony married, he and Frieda left for their spell in Mexico. Through his involvement with the Bursum Bill he had become deeply suspicious of activism on behalf of Native Americans. From Mexico, he wrote to Mabel, telling her not to 'trouble about the Indians. You can't save them: and politics, no matter what politics, will only destroy them . . . In your lust even for a Saviour's power, you would just destroy them.'

Lawrence also blasted Collier, warning that the 'salvationist but poisonous white consciousness' of the two of them was merely destructive. Three months later, he wrote that their poking and prying into the Indians was a form of indecency. What Mabel needed to do was work out her own redemption on a personal level. Anything else was merely exploiting Indian culture for the sake of her own ego.

In fact, Mabel's view was not so far from his own. Her driving interest was to comprehend and document the vast difference she felt between Native Americans and herself. After her total involvement over the Bursum Bill, she drew back from politics and pursued this interest through her writing, though her myth making about utopia still tended towards a romantic view.

Lawrence was confused in his own attitude to Native Americans. Poems written before he even reached America's shores show his apprehensive fascination. One, written in Italy, contrasts the turkey-cock, 'Like a Red Indian darkly unfinished and aloof', with a peacock.

> The peacock lifts his rods of bronze
> And struts blue-brilliant out of the far East.
> But watch a turkey prancing low on earth
> Drumming his vaulted wings, as savages drum
> Their rhythms on long-drawn, hollow, sinister drums.
> The ponderous, sombre sound of the great drum of
>   Huichilobos
> In pyramid Mexico, during sacrifice.

The poet ponders whether the turkey-cock, which has been metaphorically transformed into the aboriginal Indian, is the 'bird of the next dawn',

> The East a dead letter, and Europe moribund. . . . Is
>   that so?
> And those sombre, dead, feather-lustrous Aztecs,
>   Amerindians,
> In all the sinister splendour of their red blood-sacrifices,
> Do they stand under the dawn, half-godly, half-demon,
>   awaiting the cry of the turkey-cock?

At the same time, he was repulsed,

Your sort of gorgeousness,
Dark and lustrous
And skinny repulsive
And poppy-glossy,
Is the gorgeousness that evokes my most puzzled
   admiration.

Arriving in Taos, Lawrence was by turns admiring, supercilious, resistant and prejudiced. His essay 'Taos' shows that while observing the outward forms of the culture, he felt an unbridgeable distance from his own. The thing was visceral, 'It brings a sick sort of feeling over me, always, to get into the Indian vibration. Like breathing chlorine.' Yet although he did not want to engage, he acknowledged his deep ambivalence. His self-knowledge and honesty allowed him to examine the nature of the barrier between himself and the Indian in a way that would retain relevance for generations to follow.

Called on by Mabel to 'write the country up', he tried to please her as quickly as possible. Almost, as he might have put it, unconsciously. His essay 'Indians and an Englishman' acknowledged his bewilderment. He knew nothing, he was like a bumpkin in a circus ring. He could see no common purpose or common sympathy among the component races of the Southwest. He was expected to take sides, to be pro-Mexican or pro-Indian, art or intellect, Republican or Democrat. It was like a comic opera that took itself seriously.

To make up for his lack of comprehension, Lawrence described the outward forms of what he was seeing: what the people wore, 'the strange lines on their faces' and so forth. He references the turkey-cock, 'they give the war-whoop, like a turkey giving a startled shriek and then gobble-gobbling with laughter'. He is surprised by it, bewildered and deeply affected, 'something in my soul broke down'.

He almost loses his personal boundaries, sensing that he himself is a product of tribal consciousness and that it is still inside him somewhere, 'every drop of me trembles still alive to the old sound, every thread in my body quivers to the frenzy of the old mystery'.

Lawrence admits he may understand nothing, but he knows the old tribal way is not for him. His individualised consciousness is too important to him for any return to that past to be viable, but he sees in the tribal mysteries his own derivation, 'I was born of no Virgin Mary, of no Holy Ghost'.

Lawrence's approach to Native American culture was of a much more profound order than that of Mabel and Collier, who also tried to understand it but did not question the reasons for their difficulty. Lawrence never stopped questioning himself. Ultimately, he was able to take his own cultural baggage out of the equation long enough to see that of the Indian with clarity. His 1924 essay 'Indians and Entertainment' examines the Western approach to dramatic spectacle as one of seeking to be entertained, and contrasts it with the Indian approach, which Lawrence sees as stemming from an orientation in which there is no concept of a separate god who created man,

> The only god there is, is involved all the time in the
> dramatic wonder and inconsistency of creation. God is
> immersed, as it were, in creation, not to be separated
> or distinguished.

In the West, however, 'the spectacle is offered to us. And we sit aloft, enthroned in the Mind, dominated by some one exclusive idea, and we judge the show.' Lawrence's path to understanding the Indian approach to ritual dance and performance is to see that for the Indian there is no Onlooker, no Mind and absolutely no judgement.

In his beautiful, penetrating essays 'The Dance of the Sprouting Corn' and 'The Hopi Snake Dance', also written in 1924, he seems to write from this Indian perspective, reporting in detail the progression of the dances without offering any weighting of mediating Western perception. He writes of his feelings as he watches the dances, appreciating them in their intrinsic power and beauty.

Most of the three thousand other spectators had come to see men holding live snakes in their mouths, to see a circus performance. Lawrence saw much further. He understood the dancers did not experience the mind or spirit in an individual way. To understand the Indian way of consciousness you had to have the little ghost inside that Lawrence depicted in 'Indians and Entertainment', the little ghost which could see both ways. But even if you understood, you could not belong to both ways at once, you had to choose.

Lawrence's choice was clear, but his ranch life in New Mexico changed him in ways he did not want to forget. Back by the Mediterranean in 1925 he felt a compulsion to remember. A little drunk one evening, he writes 'A Little Moonshine with Lemon', in which he recalls with affection the ranch he named Kiowa after an old Native American trail that ran through it, and the big pine tree in front of the house.

Perhaps when I have a *Weh* at all, my *Heimweh* is for the tree in front of the house, the overshadowing tree whose green top one never looks at. But on the trunk one hangs the various odds and ends of iron things. It is so near. One goes out of the door, and the tree-trunk is there, like a guardian angel . . .

The Mediterranean, so eternally young, the very symbol of youth! And Italy, so reputedly old, yet for ever so child-like and naïve! Never, never for a moment able to comprehend the wonderful, hoary age of America, the continent of the afterwards.

As for Mabel, Lawrence regarded her too with ambivalence. On the one hand she embodied what he saw as the terrible mistake of twentieth-century women who sought freedom through emasculating men. Instead of accepting Mabel as she was, as he did the Native Americans, he decided Mabel must be saved. Thinking of inviting her to join his hoped-for utopian community, he suggested she change her dress style. Instead of loose, free-flowing garments, she should wear Mother Hubbard dresses with drawn-in waist, white stockings and an apron with matching hair ribbons. It was like putting Malvolio in yellow stockings and cross garters. Anyone who knew Mabel or had even seen a photograph of her would instantly see the mockery, yet, incomprehensibly, she complied. Next it was household chores, a woman's work that Mabel had ever avoided. Again, she was submissive, trying her hand at cooking and scrubbing floors. Surely a testament to the charismatic powers of Lawrence.

Why did he insist on Mabel remaking herself? It came back, as so often with Lawrence, to the will. The industrial wasteland of the century had resulted in a malignant growth: woman, who should be the means of focussing man's creative powers, had trained her mind to match the machines created by men. She had appropriated the male will and bent it to her own purposes. A line for an American novel he never finished perfectly describes his feeling. Of Sybil, a heroine modelled on Mabel, he writes, 'Perhaps she felt some power of her will could at last neutralise altogether the power of the engines . . . So there they would sit for ever, the train and she at a deadlock on the Santa Fe line.'

Both Lawrence and Mabel needed people around them to legitimise their role as seers. For Mabel it was the movers and shakers she brought to Taos, hoping they would immortalise her. For Lawrence it was the people he gathered around him — two Danish artists, Mabel and Brett in Taos, and also those whose views he influenced. After conversations with Lawrence, Aldous Huxley wrote about Native Americans before he had even seen any.

The Lawrences spent a final six months at the Kiowa ranch in 1925. During the whole of that sojourn, they avoided visiting Mabel, though Lawrence wrote to her. Even after he and Frieda finally left New Mexico in 1925, he continued to correspond, and not long before his death in 1930 he suggested they might 'begin a new life, with real tenderness in it'. It would have meant finding a way of sidestepping the battle of wills. As things turned out, it was a touching way of saying goodbye.

There was one other legacy left by Lawrence in Taos. The year before he died, police confiscated nine of his oil paintings from a gallery in London. The seizure did not come out of the blue. Two of his novels, *The Rainbow* and *Lady Chatterley's Lover*, had already fallen prey to attacks on his freedom of expression. The authorities considered the paintings obscene and they were shaping up for formal destruction until Lawrence secured a reprieve by agreeing to take them out of England for good. They eventually ended up at the hotel in Taos that overlooks the plaza.

The La Fonda hotel is the same vintage as the Big House itself and the owner, Saki Karavas, was an admirer of Lawrence's writing. If I had known all this in time, I could have visited the hotel and seen the paintings, as Geoff Dyer did during his own pilgrimage to Lawrentian haunts, which he wrote about in his homage with a difference, *Out of Sheer Rage*. As it was, he saw the paintings and I saw the windows.

After Lawrence's death, the battle of wills between Mabel and Frieda erupted unrestrained. Each believed they knew what Lawrence would have wanted done with his ashes: Frieda that they should be held in a little chapel on the

Kiowa ranch; Mabel that they should be scattered across its very soil. Mabel schemed to steal the urn containing the ashes, but Frieda pre-empted her by having them mixed with sand and cement in an altar block in the chapel. Mabel had no answer to that and thus the ashes lie there to this day.

Lawrence's death left Dorothy Brett bereft of the purpose for which she had come to Taos, but she stayed on. From the beginning, New Mexico seemed to liberate her from the constraints of England and the class that, as daughter of a viscount, she had been born to, but with Lawrence's death, she began to realise her potential. As she told Rudnick in an interview, 'Lawrence's ego never permitted a woman any creative ability.'[18] She became much admired as an artist, especially for her sensitive and powerful paintings of the Pueblo women's dances and of women and children.

Gradually, with her plain speech and indifference to what people thought of her, she acquired the role of village eccentric. She stayed on in Taos until her death at ninety-four. She knew not only Lawrence and Frieda, and Mabel but also O'Keeffe, Millicent Rogers and even Dennis Hopper, and so she moves through my narrative as a kind of continuity thread.

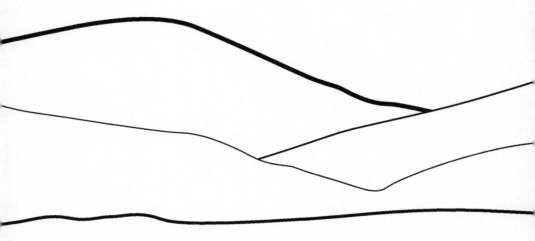

6
The Blue
Lake

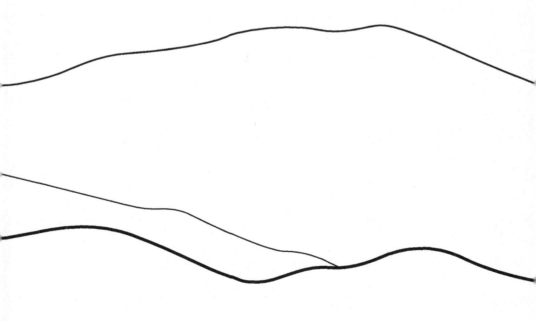

6

The Blue Lake

My next throw of the roulette dice yielded Frank Waters. Judy Gentry told me about him when the o-m and I were staying at the Big House. She told me his novels and non-fiction demonstrated a rare understanding of Native American cultures. She said he had known Mabel and Tony, and after New Mexico took hold of his imagination he lived most of the rest of his long life there. I had never heard of him and it was months later that I sat down to read his best-known novel, *The Man Who Killed the Deer*, and then to find out more about the man.

Waters was a late arrival at the Big House. His path had been preceded by the visits, engineered by Mabel, of anthropologist Elsie Clews Parsons and the psychoanalyst Carl Jung. They were part of a wave of ethnographic interest that, by the 1920s, was unstoppable.

The Pueblos had been quietly enduring for hundreds of years, managing to keep their cultures reasonably intact, despite intrusions and attack from Spanish, Mexican and then Union forces that regarded them as alien and inferior. Secrecy concerning their rituals and practices was an important part of their success, but as the Pueblo became a beacon for people critical of their own materialistic and dualistic cultures, it was more and more difficult to maintain. Many believed that these ancient peoples had things to teach them which could benefit their own societies. But a sense of entitlement characterised the entire exodus from the Old World to the new in pursuit of health and prosperity, and it was in the DNA of ethnographers too. The cultures of the indigenous peoples were at first discounted, then they were prized (by some), but either way they were under threat.

In 1921 Elsie Clews Parsons, who had helped Mabel campaign on the Bursum Bill, came to Taos and committed herself to long-term research on Pueblo culture. Mabel provided information about customs and traditions, while Tony became her loyal supporter. He was careful not to divulge anything his tribe would have considered secret, but she managed to gain privileged information from other members and painstakingly put together her material. In 1936 she published a monograph, *Taos Pueblo*, which revealed secret names and sacraments of Taos Pueblo. This was a direct attack on the source of Indian power. It was their daily habit not even to look at a person who was being discussed, let alone use their name. Instead, they would refer to a man as 'she' and a woman 'he', fearing that direct reference might diminish their power. With the publishing of their names, members of the Pueblo suffered a sense of personal violation.

Carl Jung understood that secrecy was a vital component in the Pueblos' continuing viability. On a two-week visit to Taos in 1925, he met Ochwiay Biano (Chief Mountain Lake) at the pueblo. From their conversation he realised that the Pueblo Indians' beliefs gave them a perspective that allowed them a much bigger space than the confines of their actual existence, a space where their identity as a tribe could flourish. In *Man and His Symbols* he developed such ideas, which became enormously influential.

In 1937 Frank Waters arrived in Taos. This visit marked the beginning of his life's work as an empathetic interpreter of Native American culture. His upbringing had prepared him perfectly. In Colorado Springs, where the family lived, his father, who was part Cheyenne, did whatever work was on offer, whether selling life insurance or neckties in a haberdashery, operating a cement mixer or working the damp depths of a sylvanite mine. When his father found work at a remote trading post on the Navajo Reservation, nine-year-old Frank became fascinated by the Native American belief that every sentient being, as the offspring of sacred and inviolate Mother Earth, possessed an equal right to life. This understanding, so different from the biblical idea of man's dominion over all other creatures, became an essence of his orientation to the universe.

The family wasn't able to stay very long at the trading post and Frank senior's health declined during more gruelling years at the mine. Waters was twelve when his father had to be carried home, only to die a few days later. From then on, Waters became more and more interested in his Indian roots.

Abandoning an early interest in engineering, he travelled the Southwest for years, living as a nomad and writing whatever he could sell. Upon arrival in Taos, he began frequenting the pueblo, where he met Tony Luhan, who became a kind of ceremonial uncle, playing the role of the maternal uncle who tutors his nephew in the beliefs and rituals of the pueblo. Waters became Tony's loyal defender. When he was criticised in the township for being lazy, Waters pointed out his role in overseeing the ploughing and harvesting of crops and in helping his tribe. He had also, Waters reminded people, given unstinting assistance to John Collier.

Through Tony, Waters met Mabel. Wary at first, he found her generous and kind-hearted, with a keen sense of fun. She offered him a house where he lived over the winter, and introduced him to Eastern philosophy. This started Waters on a lifelong study of the synergies between Southwest Indian and Eastern religions. He believed that if people could grasp the connection between their inner world and the cosmos, the West might be liberated from its pursuit of empty materialism at the expense of the environment. His twenty-seven books explored this theme in depth and his name was repeatedly put forward for a Nobel Prize, until his death in 1995 terminated the nominations. He dedicated his masterpiece, *The Man Who Killed the Deer*, to Mabel and Tony. It was a friendship that endured throughout their lives.

During his second visit to Taos, in 1938, Mabel and Tony offered him the room above Tony's garage, where he wrote most of *The Man Who Killed the Deer*. This novel enabled me to apprehend aspects of the American psyche in a way I hadn't before. Its protagonist, Martiniano, is selected by a government agent to be educated far away at an Indian residential school, although he is due to be initiated into the tribe's beliefs and practices. His father objects but is forced to concede under pain of a public whipping and the remonstrations of the council and the chief of the kiva fall on deaf ears. Martiniano goes away, only to return six years later to find he no longer belongs. The council won't let him take his turn at the thresher for his oats and wheat, forcing him to thresh the old, slow way, by animal hoof. That results in his missing the official hunting season, thus bringing him up against the white man's law when he hunts two days after it closes.

Although the tribe is still important to Martiniano, he has adopted some values of Western culture and is impatient with his people's resistance to modernisation. He refuses to cut off the heels of his new shoes to make them more like moccasins and prefers to irrigate his land rather than dance for rain. Nor will he cut out the seat of his trousers and wear a blanket to conceal his exposed buttocks. Whether by fine or by lash, the tribal leaders are unrelenting in their punishments, but Martiniano is extremely stubborn. He turns against both the government authorities who insisted on his learning modern American ways and the Indian Council who insist he return to the old.

In prose that often flows like poetry, Waters makes comprehensible the absence of individuality in the Native American psyche,

> They were people who so identified their lives with the one great flow of life that they showed no sense of individuality, and seemed at once impersonal and anonymous. They had attained the faculty of so obliterating themselves when gathered together in a group that even their faces lost individual expression, and looked blankly out with the one face of the tribe.[19]

It struck me that I would find it extremely threatening to look upon a sea of undifferentiated faces. My whole existence has been built upon the basis of individuality and I find it impossible to imagine who I would be if I had no sense of my own individual being. But Waters is saying that for the Native American, that very lack is a measure of belonging to the tribe. In a sense the *tribe* is the individual entity. I had come across something similar when I researched individuality in feudal England for my book on belonging. People then knew *God* as Identity, rather than their separate selves. They lived in a society that had changed very little in hundreds of years and they differentiated themselves by their role in society as peasant, artisan, knight or cleric, rather than by personality. I knew that for Maori, too, the notion of personal individuality was much less important than to Pakeha New Zealanders raised in Western traditions.

As a result of his years at the government away-school, Martiniano struggles with this absence of individuality and has to seek help from his friend Palemon. Palemon soon runs out of words, for Native Americans do not like to answer questions, nor to put their feelings into talk. Instead he radiates silent compassion. For the sake of his readers, Waters puts the sense of Palemon's intention in italics and there it is for all of us word-dependent Westerners to see. On earth, Palemon tells Martiniano, he is imprisoned in his mortal body and has to learn to live with its needs and limitations and how to supersede them. He is also imprisoned in the 'greater body' — of his tribe, his pueblo, his people — and there too he learns to live with its needs and limitations and how to supersede them.

Palemon understands that Martiniano's way must be different: *his* 'greater body' is a form of life which rejects both the old ways and some of the white man's new ones. He will have to find his own path and how to live harmoniously within it. Then his spirit will be able to 'become one with the flowing stream of all life, everlasting, formless and without bounds'. He will be free.

For killing a deer outside the hunting season in the now government-owned National Forest, Martiniano must either be fined or go to gaol. That's white man's law. For failing to seek the deer's permission first, he must also be punished. It's not that the Indian way forbids killing — one life must sometimes give way to another so that 'the one great life of all may continue unbroken' — but there is a right way and a wrong way. The life of the deer is as precious as their own and both are children of the same source, all one life on the same Mother Earth. If permission is sought, the life of the deer will continue in the Indian's life and, in turn, in the one life all around him and the deer will be content. But in Martiniano's case, the deer's permission was not sought and the Indian Council was anguished, 'What have we done to this deer, our brother? What have we done to ourselves?' It is vital that the members of the council move in unison together.

Finally they decide that Martiniano should be brought to justice in the white man's court and that the punishment will cover both aspects of his wrongdoing. He is sentenced to three months in gaol or a fine of $150.

Martiniano realises he needs a faith more in line with his revised values than that espoused by the kiva, which advocates passivity before nature, as in dancing for rain rather than digging trenches. He turns to the Native American church which has revived a centuries-old practice of using a hallucinogen-containing cactus, peyote, for spiritual enlightenment. The US Government had banned its use, thus making it irresistible as a way for Native Americans to assert their way of life against the authorities.

Martiniano eventually finds his own way and his own brand of faith in a blend of traditional Indian and modern American. He comes to understand and value the ritual dances but will participate in them only at the bidding of his own spirit and not at the behest of the tribe. In this way he retains an essence of individuality and freedom. The old men of the tribe are content.

The Man Who Killed the Deer liberated a shift in my consciousness that went deeper and broader than the simple story. It helped me understand the indigenous people of my own country better. Although, in the past 180 years, many of the old Maori ways have been brutally impacted by colonisation, there are still striking resonances with some of the values mentioned in the novel. A couple I have experienced directly are a preference not to look people of authority in the eye and a resistance to being confronted by direct questions. As a teacher and the daughter of a Yorkshire-born-and-bred mother, I needed to be reassured that these customs were not a sign of disrespect.

Also shared is a resistance to certain kinds of change, those that conflict with traditional values. I once argued with a respected New Zealand author for humility before nature. We were discussing the logging of trees. Karl asked, somewhat mockingly, Will it help if you ask the tree first? and I, feeling a little foolish, replied, Yes.

After reading Waters I felt that when I met another Native American I would be able to communicate, and even if it was only with silence that would be fine. He also gave me a new metaphor with which to interpret the snow I'd seen falling outside the Big House on our last day there. Martiniano describes how the world is changed by snow.

> It looked like a loose feather dropped from the breast of a solitary wild goose. It twisted and turned buoyantly against the blue mountain wall, fluttered down lazily past the brown adobe wall, settled lightly on the hard reddish earth. Another. Others. They came! They came! The mystery, the miracle, the beauty of the first snow.
>
> By morning it was all gone. The sun was bright, the air warm. But the message of a new mystery, new miracle and new beauty remained.[20]

Once the snow comes, the people must move in from their huts in the fields and canyon and stay still together.

There must be no digging within the pueblo walls, no plastering or chopping of wood. No singing, no dancing, no hair cutting either. Women must clean their houses and do their noisy sweeping only after sundown, and then it was best to place a live coal near the door. No automobiles were allowed in the plaza. Wood could be brought in on burros only. It was the time of staying still. Our Mother Earth sleeps.[21]

There is something liberating in the idea of snow guiding the people and of the people accepting her guidance. While Mother Earth sleeps, life prepares for its renewal, when Mother Earth will fling off her blanket and lie open to sun and rain in readiness for new abundance. It's not that I believe this message of the snow in a concrete way; it's more that it opens me to the idea of humankind living in harmony with nature, being responsive and respectful, gaining peace and fulfilment through it. This, I think, is what Waters wanted to offer to people of both races: the possibility of carrying over values of the Native Americans that could help heal the destructiveness of modern American life.

As Rodolfo Byers, the Indian trader in the novel, says, 'The brotherhood of man! It will always be a dreary phrase, a futile hope, until each man, all men, realise that they themselves are but different reflections and insubstantial images of a greater invisible whole.'[22] Byers believes it is the cry of every human heart to find a way to span the wordless chasm that separates us all. This is what Waters wanted too.

It took sixty-four years of struggle, from 1906 to 1970, for the Pueblo to gain full title to the sacred Blue Lake. In 1933 Congress granted a special-use permit for 13,000 hectares surrounding it, but the public still had right of access and unfortunately some among them discarded their litter or threw their old fish bait into the lake as they passed through, which strengthened the tribe's resolve to stop at nothing less than full title. By the time they achieved their final victory, they had learned many tools of trade for dealing with governments of the day.

The Man Who Killed the Deer dramatises this battle over the Blue Lake (Dawn Lake in the novel). As in reality, the Pueblo characters never lose sight of the return of the land as their main objective. When the district superintendent asks why the Indians are giving all this trouble, first about the deer that was killed and by then insisting on making peyote central to their new religion, the chiefs answer, 'What about that land which is ours but still withheld from us?' They mean the Blue Lake.

As a compromise, the government allows the use of peyote in Native American church ceremonies, but compromise doesn't interest the Indians, who repeat, Give us back our sacred lake. They refuse to discuss anything but 'the greater things'. They want one place where they can be themselves, free to sing and dance and worship as they will. They maintain their secrecy about their spiritual practices.

Waters arrived in Taos a year after Parsons published her monograph *Taos Pueblo*, and he brought the Pueblos' feelings of outrage to life in his novel. 'There in print, like letters of fire, like fingers pointing, like voices shouting, were the names of the kivas, their own names.'[23] Even their Dawn Lake was mentioned.

Tony came under suspicion of being one of the informants and the relationship between Parsons and the Luhans grew cool. The Pueblo punished some of the suspected informants and intensified its demands for the return of the Blue Lake. Its members turned against the white people who sometimes walked into their houses and mocked their way of life. They didn't want any more picnicking under the trees leaving rubbish and dirtying the streams. Dissension grew until the district superintendent had *Taos Pueblo* withdrawn from sale in New Mexico. A land board of three men examined the land claims, but found that the amount of money required to provide compensation would be astronomical. The Pueblo chiefs stuck to their demands.

Their special-use permit was due to run out in 1983, but the uproar was so great and so many Americans had come to appreciate the needs and rights of their indigenous population that enlightened change was now possible. With President Nixon to the fore, outright ownership of the entire 19,000 hectares including the Blue Lake was returned to the Pueblo in perpetuity in 1970.

To be accurate, it was not just President Nixon, not a matter of one individual making a good decision, but the culmination of concerted effort. In the 1960s a new identity politics was being forged by Black Power, the American Indian movement, women's liberation and gay rights. The people of Taos Pueblo capitalised on their hard-won political experience by approaching Senator Harris, whose wife LaDonna was of Comanche descent. After meeting the Taos Pueblo chiefs, they were in sympathy with their cause and it became their mission to get the Pueblo its land back 'if it's the one thing we do'.

LaDonna Harris brought an Indian approach to her model of advocacy, which was summed up in an article as 'I Interact, Therefore I Am'.[24] For her, relationships were of paramount importance, not only in her personal life but also in negotiations, no matter what the scale. The relationships she forged during the campaign enabled the Pueblo claim to become truly bipartisan and proved crucial in its success. At the same time Senator Harris worked through formal political channels, promoting the bill as a signal that 'henceforth the Congress will devote its efforts to uplifting Indian pride and competence, to confirming the strengths of their "Indian-ness,", and to encouraging Indians to find their place in American society as Indians'.

It was the first time indigenous identity had been addressed in Congress. Assisted by a national letter-writing campaign and imaginative publicity stunts, hundreds of feature articles and editorials about the Blue Lake claim appeared around the country. Finally, the Senate voted seventy to twelve to give the whole 19,000 hectares back to Taos Pueblo and President Nixon signed the bill into law. It brought much closer Frank Waters' dream of Indians becoming part of the national commonwealth, and the Pueblo honours Nixon for it to this day.

7
Big Fat Secret in the High Desert

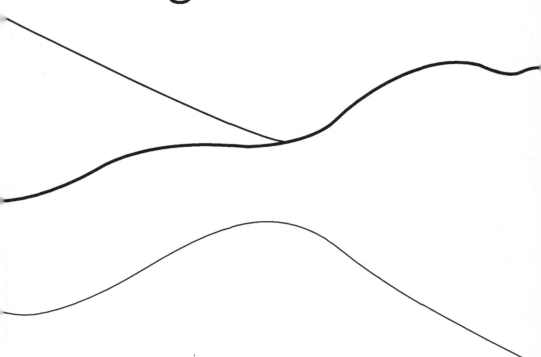

It was wise of the o-m, when the bus to Santa Fe passed by Los Alamos, to do nothing more than point out the location of the town. I stared at him as realisation dawned that in coming to see a wilder, less commercialised America, I had arrived at a cradle for ultimate destruction. It settled in my mind like a succubus, at odds with all by which I wanted to define the desert. I could not bear to think about it while I was in New Mexico. Safely back in Wellington, I could ignore reality no longer and reluctantly took to the internet.

During World War II the potential of radioactivity for arms became apparent. Scientists in Berlin discovered that by splitting the atom into two elements, they could create a mass greater than the sum of its parts. By 1942 the war had gone on so long and with such carnage and suffering that finding a way to end it had become a consuming passion. The US Government looked about for a site remote enough to make secrecy possible and found Los Alamos. It was deemed suitable for a top secret undertaking on account of its small population and a boys' ranch school that could provide instant accommodation for the scientists. The boys dispersed, the school was closed, the scientists and their entourage moved in. Within a year, the population of Los Alamos was up to 3500 and by the end of 1944 it had reached 5700. The deadly bombs exploded over Japan in 1945 were a direct result of the scientists' work in Los Alamos.

As a culture, the town was of course peculiar. Everyone in Los Alamos had a job, because you couldn't get a house unless you were connected with the laboratory or the maintenance company. All employees had to wear an identification badge which they flashed upon entering or leaving one of the technical buildings. Many of them also wore a piece of film that registered radiation exposure. It was checked once a month and if it indicated excessive exposure, the employee was transferred to another position. Residents were not allowed to build their own homes or participate in any kind of local self-government.

It was not until I found Frank Waters' novel *The Woman at Otowi Crossing* that I began to think seriously about how the Manhattan Project had affected the lives of both the scientists and the peoples of the desert. Waters wrote it first in the early 1950s while working as an information consultant for the Los Alamos Scientific Laboratory, but it was rejected by publisher after publisher until at last he found one in 1966. It's easy to read but some of the notions are difficult to get into one's head, or at least *this* head. Waters rewrote it several times and even then was not entirely satisfied. He wrote to Alan Swallow, who was to publish it,

Finally, I realised you just can't fake anything, successful as it might at first appear. You have to accept your own premise. We all live two lives, separated by the Psychical Iron Curtain that makes us all schizophrenic, but they meet and blend in our daily actions as plain people. So I at last did the natural thing: let the Woman epitomise one pole of our dual nature, counterpointing the extroverted scientific process of nuclear fission, and throwing her into perspective against the other characters . . .

What I would hope for is that the novel will go down easily, like a sugar pill, so that its implicit meanings will dissolve and begin to work. In other words, that the book will not be immediately exhausted but take hold of the imagination . . .[25]

The story brings the settlement to life through the character of Edmund Gaylord. As a young physics major in New York who had just obtained his PhD and was expecting to undergo more years of teaching and scrimping to pay off his debts, Gaylord was offered a job in Chicago. He wasn't told the exact nature of the work except that it was scientifically important to the war effort. He was set to work in an empty room containing a pile of bricks. Two kinds of bricks – graphite and uranium. This was the raw material from which the men were to design a gun-type nuclear chain reactor.

Gaylord and his forty-one colleagues painstakingly built up alternate layers of the bricks with a grey balloon cloth shrouding all but one side. The graphite engulfed them daily, releasing them at the end of their shifts looking like coalminers or performers in a minstrel show. It also permeated their skin. Working against time, they erected a huge cube, which they called simply 'the pile'. As it gained in volume, the balloon cloth removed the neutron-capturing air. Eventually the uranium became almost a critical mass, enough to initiate a self-sustaining reaction. Through repeated experiment, they managed to initiate – and then halt – the world's first self-sustaining nuclear reaction.

After that success, the work gathered momentum.

Gaylord, no longer a novice, was brought to Los Alamos, a heap so far of old log cabins, ramshackle prefabs and army barracks being thrown up by a construction crew. He was under orders to tell no one where he was going. The only address he could give people was PO Box 1663. If he needed a driver's licence, income tax returns, food and petrol ration books or an insurance policy, he had to clear it through the security office. He must not visit any local community alone and was discouraged from having any member of his family come within 160 kilometres. Gaylord accepted all the strictures, but it wasn't long before he fell in love with Emily, daughter of the woman of the title and an anthropologist who had returned to New Mexico to finish her dissertation, and then of course felt guilty when he went to visit her.

Inside the compound, as the methodology brought the production of the reactor to a critical point, the scientists were painfully aware of the danger they were in and the high stakes of getting it wrong. People living nearby gradually became aware that something strange was happening. They might see a brilliant flash of light spurting into the sky, followed by a sharp crack and a rumble echoing across the hills. They thought it might be from a factory for windshield wipers in submarines or a home for mothers-to-be from the Women's Army Corps or a concentration camp for socialists.

The desert and its peoples were subject to more unnatural wonders when the world's first nuclear test was carried out 120 kilometres south of Albuquerque in Socorro County. The scientists had moved on from the gun-type reactor, which used a great deal of uranium, to developing the more sophisticated implosion type, which used much less, and they needed to know it would successfully detonate following impact. Robert Oppenheimer, director of the Los Alamos lab, gave the test the code name Trinity, which he later said was inspired by some John Donne poetry that was in his head at the time. There is a line that goes, 'Batter my heart, three person'd God'.

The only building in the vicinity of the test site was the McDonald Ranch House complex which the government had already acquired, but preparations were made to evacuate surrounding ranches and isolated communities if the radioactivity became too high, while all the access roads were blocked. The test took place at 5.29am. It gouged a crater a metre and a half deep and nine metres wide, transforming the desert sand into radioactive, light green glass, which later came to be called Trinitite. The surrounding mountains were illuminated 'brighter than daytime' for a couple of seconds and the heat was reported as 'hot as an oven' at the base camp. It was felt over 160 kilometres away, easily encompassing Taos, Santa Fe and O'Keeffe's home in Abiquiu. A mushroom-shaped cloud emerged above the observers and far beyond, reaching twelve kilometres in height.[26]

A witness later wrote that upon detonation, the groups of people who had been standing 'rooted to the earth like desert plants broke into dance, the rhythm of primitive man dancing at one of his fire festivals at the coming of Spring'. And again, Oppenheimer was ready with a holy metaphor, this time remembering a verse from the Bhagavad-Gita, 'if the radiance of a thousand suns were to burst at once into the sky, that would be like the splendour of the mighty one'.[27]

This bomb, nicknamed Fat Man because of its spherical shape, was dropped over Nagasaki three weeks later, killing an estimated 60-80,000 people. Little Boy had already devastated Hiroshima by then, killing 66,000 and many more in the following months. A new age had dawned and the world had become a vastly more dangerous place, but few people at the time had any idea of what was happening in the desert around them.

One person who did have a deeper understanding of the

forces being unleased was Edith Warner, a white woman who ran a small café beside the Rio Grande. She had come to the Otowi Crossing in 1928 and grown close to the Native American people. As the Manhattan Project progressed, she also came to know some of the physicists from the secret society on the hill and her house was chosen as their sanctuary outside the compound.

Waters' fictionalised version of Warner, Helen Chalmers, is likewise gifted with intuition and the perception of an identity greater than human individuality. When she discovers a lump in her breast she fears cancer and this catapults her into a reassessment of her life and what, if anything, it means. Although her doctor is reassuring, she feels as if her life has been useless. Then suddenly she experiences something like 'a cataclysmic explosion that burst asunder the shell of the world around her, revealing its inner reality with its brilliant flash'.[28] She comprehends the unity of the universe, including all space and time. She emerges from the experience as a new being quite apart from the elements that had formed her. Her mind, body and spirit are now integrated with the universe in an entirely new way.

When Japan is bombed, Helen has a nightmare from which she wakes screaming. It is as if 'everything, house, mountains, the world, the heavens, was enveloped in one brilliant apocalyptic burst of fire'.[29] When the secret comes out and she realises her dream was of the bombing, she doesn't move for three days. She cannot bear the reality of all the killing or think of such life-giving power being used for death and destruction. She slowly realises that it had come from the mysterious power within man himself. The power she had felt at the time of her first vision had 'now been manifested in the outer world. Like her, mankind would suffer a period of fear and guilt. Then this would pass, and the world would face a new age with a new power to use for good.'[30] Thus Waters brings both the scientific discoveries at Los Alamos and Helen's personal psychic explosion into the same frame, suggesting their convergence with Buddhist and Indian awareness.

Gaylord gets to know Helen well. He listens attentively to her talk of 'vast projections from the soul of humanity' which nothing can finally withstand, not even the more and more powerful bombs that are being built. World opinion, she says, is a more powerful deterrent to world war than nuclear arsenals, so Gaylord writes a series of papers in which he explores the myth of the Woman at Otowi Crossing. He looks for similarities between the development and first test detonation of the atomic bomb, and the psychic phenomenon experienced by Helen Chalmers. As with the bomb, Helen has 'a sense of blinding brightness, of a great fissioning within her, a sudden fusion of her faculties'. Then an unbroken stillness envelops her. Her inner self is transformed into a new spiritual entity with greater powers of comprehension.

Does this go down like a sugar pill? Not quite.

After the war, the development and the testing continue at a new site in Nevada. Las Vegas, catering for the boys' time off, becomes the fabled play-town it is today. On one occasion, Helen and Emily, accompanied by Helen's Native American assistant Facundo, are driving from Arizona back to Otowi Crossing via the Grand Canyon. When they reach Utah a warning comes over the radio that a radioactive cloud is moving east-southeast towards southern Utah, northern Arizona and the Grand Canyon. They are told to close the car windows. Soon afterwards they are told that the mushroom cloud will be passing overhead. They are advised to go indoors and stay there until further notice. They must not drink water exposed to the air or eat food that has been left exposed.

Helen and her companions find a motel and a little later Helen's friend Turner arrives and checks into the motel across the road, but neither party can venture across to be with the other. Americans begin to understand that they have entered the Atomic Age and there is no going back. Turner, a journalist, documents a new 'Atomic' hair-do on offer from a beauty parlour along with tourists coming to see the explosions. He reports that the ABC of the children of scientists and construction workers at the base now begins with A is for Atom, B is for Bomb, C is for Careful.

These descriptions enabled me to imagine ordinary people being impacted by radioactivity in the course of their daily lives, and I was puzzled to realise I felt more intimately affected than when I learned as a teenager of Hiroshima and Nagasaki. The nature of death and the numbers there were so horrendous I found them unfathomable.

I once met a person who had survived Hiroshima and had spent her later life as a travelling lecturer to ensure such horror was never repeated. Bun (pronounced as in carbon) took me to the emperor's shrine in Tokyo, where trees were exploding with the reds, rusts, yellows of autumn, and we talked about her life, including that day in Hiroshima. Could I imagine the magnitude of the terror and suffering the people went through? No, I absolutely couldn't. Could anyone *imagine* it?

Could such infliction of suffering ever be justified? I wanted to know what the o-m thought. He was a very humane person. The photographs of Iraqi soldiers being slaughtered in the Gulf War filled him with anguish and the only quarrel we ever had arose over an interpretation of humanity. It happened after we had left New Mexico and were crossing the Golden Gate bridge in a bus, discussing a book by Joan Didion, *The Year of Magical Thinking*. The o-m said he lost all sympathy for Didion when she refused to let her husband's eyes be used for research. I stood up for Didion, telling the o-m of how my own children had not wanted me to donate my eyes either, though they would be happy with donations of my other organs.

The o-m suddenly became furious, 'I'd have thought they had more humanity.' I jumped to their defence and then we both took refuge in angry silence.

The o-m's view about the bombing of Hiroshima disturbed me for another reason. He said it was easy now, from the upholstered comfort of over fifty years, to condemn the bombing of Hiroshima, but decisions like this were not made in a moral vacuum. In 1945, after over five years of war that had enveloped people all over the world, there was an overwhelming sense of weariness. Japan was uncompromisingly expansionist. Australia was scared witless and even New Zealanders had built bunkers at North Head in Auckland. The Americans had suffered casualties in the hundreds of thousands as their forces attempted to make their way to Japan via the heavily defended islands of the Pacific.

Dropping a newly developed bomb on Japan was seen as a way to stop the never-ending haemorrhage of Allied casualties. The bombing of Nagasaki was far less defensible, he said.

When I found myself so close to the test site in the desert, I realised how inadequately I had come to terms with the fact of the destruction and suffering wreaked upon others far away. The o-m's words didn't reconcile me to the bombing, but they made me realise the difficulty of judging. How can I know if fear would not have changed my own consciousness to a point where fatal, indiscriminate retaliation seemed justified? As I ask myself these questions for the hundredth time, I find unexpectedly that I'm starting to leave the fear and guilt behind.

8

Conquistadors
in the Saddle

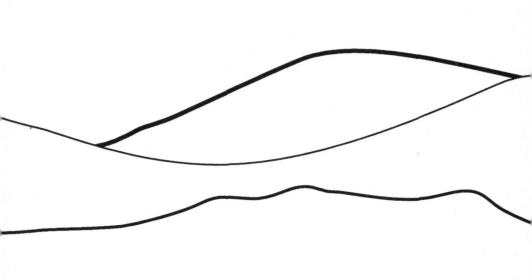

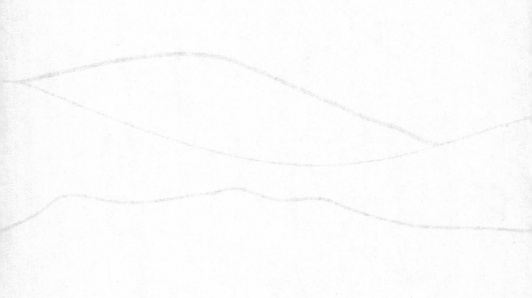

It was snowing when the o-m and I left Taos and it was still snowing when we arrived in Santa Fe. The driver told us to stay on the bus so he could drop us right outside the hotel, a kindness I put down to the o-m effect. It was a Hilton of a more personalised kind than I was used to. In the lounge area beside reception were an open fire and comfortable armchairs where you could truly lounge and read newspapers.

Shockingly, there had been a massacre in Paris. Gunmen and suicide bombers had hit, almost simultaneously, a concert hall, a major stadium, restaurants and bars. I read that 130 people had been killed and hundreds wounded. The attackers were Islamic extremists but for me the most disturbing fact was that they were Europeans. The *Independent* said the Brussels suburb where several of the attackers lived was 'a melting pot of malign elements'. Over the years I had nurtured the idea that, unlike America, Europe was a safe and sane place. Now I knew it wasn't.

As we chomped through our American signature sand-wiches of ham, bacon, processed cheese, lettuce, mayo and tomato held together on a stick, the o-m helped me get a historical perspective on the country's gun laws. Early settlers defending their settlements in the wilderness depended on their guns. The American Revolutionary War was waged and won with guns – guns fired not only by the Continental Army but also by part-time civilian soldiers who formed militias in each colony.

After the war, the Continental Army was disbanded – Americans viewed standing armies with deep distrust. Instead the tradition of militias of armed civilians was written into the Constitution in its famous Second Amendment. The phrase 'right to bear arms' envisaged an army of territorial soldiers who kept their weapons at home. 'Very like the Swiss Army', said the o-m, which allowed soldiers to keep their guns, *not* including ammunition, at home. Instead, the Constitution was interpreted to mean that *every person*, not just a designated militia, had the right to carry a gun.

Of all the states, New Mexico had the longest history of violence and the longest period as a frontier. During discussions after our return home, the o-m took the word 'frontier' and contrasted its pioneering connotation in New Zealand history with the US where it was always associated with lawlessness. Again, he compared the US with Switzerland, where the guns were service rifles, whereas in the States, handguns like the Colt, with its six-shooter-chamber holding the rounds, became popular. The o-m said this was where the curse was. Mention of the Colt brought back a long-forgotten memory of a childhood game in the fields behind our house in Surrey, 'That's what we used to play cowboys and Indians with!'

Our plan was to stay in Santa Fe overnight and the next day wander through the town, look at the art shops, visit the cathedral, the Palace of the Governors and the O'Keeffe

Museum, before catching a train for Albuquerque at 5pm.

The o-m awoke with an idea. He would buy me a pair of leather boots for Christmas. He took my arm in his excitement, 'Sometimes I have an idea that is exactly right.' I was pleased of course, though I wasn't sure whether his idea came from love or from wanting an excuse to buy something that was quintessentially New Mexico: boots were worn by cowboys, boots were for urging horses to move faster across the lumpy terrain, they were for wading through mud and snow.

Not the ones I liked though. These were elegance personified and perhaps this was what the o-m was after too. He loved style and his gear was always top quality. We found a shop with a superb collection but the prices ranged from US$1200 to 3000. That was beyond the imagination, let alone the pocket, so we dropped the idea and found a café for lunch. This time we went Mexican. I stoked up on refried bean burritos, while the o-m refuelled with slow-cooked beef enchiladas.

In the afternoon we crossed the plaza to see the Palace of the Governors, a pleasing period building with thick adobe walls and vigas coming out over the long veranda. To me 'Palace of the Governors' sounded like a contradiction in terms. Palaces were for royalty. Governors were functionaries. This palace had begun as the seat of government in New Mexico for the conquistadors, who had been gradually infiltrating the American Southwest ever since Hernan Cortes and his cavalry appeared to astonished Aztecs as mythical beasts, half man, half dog.

Spanish interest in the region began when the conquistadors heard Indians talk about 'seven cities of gold'. No doubt it seemed like a no brainer to locate and claim the gold for themselves. From 1540 to 42, Francisco Vazquez de Coronado led an expedition to find them. When the expedition resulted in total failure, the men returned to

Mexico, but fifty years later a new set of conquistadors led by Don Juan de Onate arrived, bringing with them Franciscan missionaries. For colonisation to be worthwhile, they required two main attributes: rich mineral deposits and/or arable land plus a settled indigenous population capable of supplying tribute and labour to the colonists. Onate knew that the region had the second and hoped to be lucky with the first.

In 1598, with Spain's official approval, he succeeded in founding New Mexico's first Spanish province, Santa Fe of New Mexico. It included the present-day states of Texas, Arizona, Utah, Colorado, Nevada and California as well as modern New Mexico.

As the o-m and I wandered through the Palace of the Governors, a memory from my school days infiltrated my thoughts. Spain and Portugal divided up the New World between them! I remembered staring at a map with a vertical red line cutting through countries and oceans showing which bits Spain would have and which bits would be Portuguese. They agreed not to colonise any lands with a Christian king. At school the doings of the Spaniards and Portuguese had come across as no more than a prelude to the thoroughly enlightened mighty British Empire; the peoples who happened to live in the Americas and Africa seemed impossibly remote. Now I marvelled at the arrogance of that lordly division and groaned for the peoples robbed of freedom.

In one of the rooms I spied a model of the pueblo at Acoma. Willa Cather tells a story of this pueblo in *Death Comes for the Archbishop* so I made a beeline for it. The model depicted adobe dwellings erected on a 111-metre mesa, with the only access a series of almost vertical steps cut into the rock face. I could see at once what an amazing site for a stronghold it was, yet at the same time how vulnerable to the enemy once it was on the mesa. Indeed, in a bid to quell the resistance, Onate's conquistadors had stormed the pueblo and amputated the right foot of twenty-four of their prisoners. The Acoma were then exploited for their labour and resources, while the Franciscans who tried to convert them forfeited respect because of their own demands for food, clothing and labour.

In her novel Cather recounts the legend of Fray Baltazar, the resident priest of Acoma. He appropriated the best of the people's crops and sheep, made the women water his garden and forced the men to give their labour in tribute to his church. In this, he was probably not unusual among the missionaries. Eventually the people turned against him and threw him off the cliff.

Onate's hopes of finding minerals suitable for mining came to nothing and he also found little fertile land for agriculture. The place didn't seem to merit colonisation, so in 1607 he resigned his governorship and abandoned New Mexico altogether.

He was replaced by Pedro de Peralta, who in 1610 based his capital in Santa Fe and began construction of the palace. He encouraged missions to bring religious enlightenment to the native population and to manage the agricultural industry. The Indians, however, hated the Spanish prohibition of their own religion and the encomienda system that was put in place. This system, the brainchild of the Spanish Crown, gave colonists in America the right to demand tribute and forced labour from the Indian inhabitants of an area.

The native population succumbed to European diseases and began to decline, an outcome common to colonisation stories everywhere. This left the civil government competing with the Franciscans for a diminishing pool of labour. A subsequent governor tried to defeat the Franciscans by forbidding them to enslave Indians. He gave the Pueblos permission to practise their traditional dances and religious ceremonies and forbade his clerics to punish them. The

Catholic Church was so powerful, however, almost like another arm of the Spanish government, that when the Franciscans complained, the governor and his assistant were handed over to the Inquisition.

Under the yoke of Franciscan rule, the Pueblo Indians, who lived on about seventy different pueblos, became so frustrated that in 1680 they rebelled. In an action orchestrated from Taos, they sacked Santa Fe and drove the Spanish back to Mexico. It was the first significant challenge to Spanish rule.

The Pueblos destroyed symbols of Catholicism and Spanish culture, including livestock and fruit trees, and resumed their religious rituals. But quarrels among the Pueblos as to who should occupy Santa Fe and rule over the territory weakened their authority so much that in 1692 when returning Spanish forces led by Diego de Vargas surrounded Santa Fe they surrendered. They swore allegiance to the King of Spain and once more took up Christianity.

Keen to avoid another expulsion, the Spanish were more reasonable this time around. In addition to giving each Pueblo substantial land grants, they appointed a public defender to protect Indian rights and argue their legal cases in the Spanish courts. They also scaled down their efforts to eliminate native culture and religion.

For many decades Mexico continued as a colony of Spain, but with diminishing popularity. The people especially hated Spain's edict against trading with Native Americans. Eventually Mexico waged a successful revolution and in 1821 declared independence, ushering New Mexico into a fresh phase of its history. As its rulers changed from Spanish to Mexican, its Spanish subjects had to adapt to seeing themselves as Mexican nationals.

Mexico opened for trade immediately and Americans were quick to take advantage. A Missouri trader named William

Becknell set out that same year for Santa Fe, creating in the process of his journey the Santa Fe Trail. New Mexico became a trading hub between the United States and Mexico. It facilitated travel by stagecoach and also enabled emigrants to get to the gold rushes in California and Colorado.

Meanwhile, the West had become irresistible to many Americans. It was convenient to believe they had a God-given right to expand westward regardless of who might be in the way. Many believed they could conquer the people already living on the land and take it for the United States. A Democratic editor coined the phrase 'manifest destiny', which made it sound eminently reasonable. Although by no means everyone believed in manifest destiny, it was cleverly marketed and carried the inestimable advantage of justifying expansion at any price.

In 1846 President Polk used a border incident as a pretext for the war he wanted with Mexico. Polk sent Colonel Kearny and his 1600 men along the Santa Fe Trail to occupy New Mexico and California. Kearny entered Santa Fe without opposition and established a joint civil and military government, forcing the Mexican authorities to retreat south to Mexico.

Now the inhabitants of New Mexico were expected to adapt to being American nationals, and many resented that. The new provisional governor, Charles Bent, tried in vain to persuade US army officers to 'respect the rights of the inhabitants' and predicted 'serious consequences' if abuses went unchecked. A year after the invasion, there was a popular uprising that became known as the Taos Revolt, in which Governor Bent and other leaders and officials were killed.

After the revolt was subdued, Mexico ceded all its territory in the American Southwest and California to the United States. As more Anglos came to live there, the Hispanos found themselves regarded as lazy and backward, with only the whitest among them considered acceptable. In 1912 the territory became the newest state in the USA.

Hidden in this story is the part played by Antonio José Martinez, whose portrait I spied in the palace. He too had featured in *Death Comes for the Archbishop*. According to the text beneath the painting, the padre played a key role in the period of transition from Mexican to US territory and was an exceptional philosopher, educator, printer and revolutionary.

'Oh,' I exclaimed to the o-m, 'but in *Death Comes for the Archbishop*, he's corrupt, licentious and backward!' The text for Archbishop Jean Lamy's portrait was only a little less worrying, describing him as 'quick to action'. As Cather painted him, Father Latour was reflective, saw different points of view and preferred to ignore things he wanted to change until conditions were more favourable. I knew I would need to try to resolve these paradoxes.

There were further questions raised by this visit to the museum. It started me thinking about the people we call Hispanos — those, like Martinez, whose Spanish ancestors came to New Mexico during those years before its incorporation into the United States. At that time they held a privileged position in society. This gradually eroded as they became a minority, with all that meant for their language and culture, and as they found themselves regarded as inferior to white Americans, they began to cling to memories of former greatness. They selected particular anniversaries, such as that of Diego de Vargas' re-entry into Santa Fe in 1692. Every year Hispanos celebrated this victory over Native Americans, dressing up as conquistadors and riding through the town on horses. They also erected statues and murals honouring their conquistadors. Onate, de Vargas and others were used as street names and their images adorned official seals and emblems. Conquistador re-enactors regularly visited schools. Even moving truck firms and a league baseball team used the image.

For many years Native American groups protested, to little effect, despite an action against a statue of Onate that saw an electric saw put paid to his right foot. This action was cheered by the people of Acoma Pueblo when they heard of it, but as a new foot was attached to the statue, the director of the Onate Monument and Visitors Centre was unsympathetic, 'Give me a break — it was 400 years ago.'

Things have changed. In 2018 the traditional pageant for the de Vargas anniversary, 'Entrada', was replaced with gestures of reconciliation, starting it off with a Catholic Mass and a performance by Pueblo dancers. Hispanic and Native American civic leaders have acknowledged 'wounds older and deeper than any on this continent'. The University of New Mexico is looking at a new design for its official seal and the school visits by conquistador re-enactors are to be regulated.

As for the Palace of the Governors, it somehow survived the Pueblo sacking of Santa Fe in 1680, but later fell into disrepair. In 1909 it became the state's first museum and a young archaeologist, Jesse Nusbaum, was hired to oversee its restoration. Looking back to the building's beginnings he decided he wanted its architecture to blend with the environment. From the beginning it had embodied adaptation to New Mexico's climate and atmosphere and its colours had echoed those of earth and sky. Now he reinforced those elements in Pueblo Revival-style architecture. It is the oldest continuously occupied building in the US.

After the Palace of the Governors, we made for the cathedral, only to find it closed. It was to have been the highlight of the day. That it was shut was my disappointment; that it was French was the o-m's. The building owed nothing to Native American or Mexican architecture.

Death Comes for the Archbishop had made me feel as Father

Latour had felt, how he had missed his native country and wanted to bring something of it to the design for the cathedral. But he loved his adopted country too. In the desert, he had happened upon a hill of a colour entirely different from that of the surrounding rock. Golden yellow, it had reminded him of the stone near his native Clermont. He picked up a chip from the rock and held it softly. He knew that this was the stone for his cathedral. As for style, he wanted Midi Romanesque, the style he had left behind in Clermont.

As readers, we are not party to the toil of the cathedral's being built, but at the end of his life the Archbishop comes to Santa Fe for the last time and is disappointed to find the town changed. In 1888, though half the plaza square was still adobe, he found the other half filled with flimsy wooden buildings, double porches and scrollwork. Quite wrong for the cathedral. Wrapped in Indian blankets, he waited for sunset when the cathedral would shine like gold.

One of the things he loved best was its position in the landscape. Just behind it were steep rose-coloured hills, so that from the end of the street it seemed to leap out of the hills, filled with spiritual purpose and action. It reminded his French architect, Molny, of churches in Italy or in the opera. More than once, Molny brought the Bishop to look at the unfinished building when a storm was coming up. The Bishop watched as the sky above the mountain darkened, while the rocks took on a lavender hue. The entire horizon seemed to come menacingly close. The cathedral had become an integral part of its surroundings in a way that would only intensify with time. Yet, Cather remarks sadly, no one but Molny and the Archbishop ever seemed to appreciate this.

This was the o-m's point, I suppose; he saw the cathedral as alien to the landscape and culture of both Native American and Mexican. He would have preferred something that reflected those cultures, or perhaps just the Native American, as Mabel's house in Taos did. Years later, not long before he died, he would recall his opinion of the cathedral, 'I can't forgive the man for building it in that foreign style.'

It felt wrong that we were barred from entry. Our communication with Archbishop Lamy was rudely terminated and pilgrims can't wait about, especially those with a train to catch. But this was the cathedral built by Father Latour — I mean Archbishop Lamy. My main purpose in coming to Santa Fe was to see it. Manifest destiny. How *could* it be closed?

We wandered away, past the cathedral grounds with their snow-laden trees, down the street to the O'Keeffe Museum, a repository for fifty O'Keeffe paintings which the o-m was extremely keen to see. At home he had an impressive collection of original art works by New Zealand artists such as Ralph Hotere, Toss Woollaston, Olivia Spencer Bower and others. One of his most cherished achievements during his time as chief archivist at Archives New Zealand was the purchase of some impressive New Zealand artwork which can still be seen through the windows as the bus goes by.

I loved looking at art with him and had looked forward to viewing the O'Keeffes, but now I was torn. On the way to the museum we had passed Native American artists and artisans displaying and selling their works from the pavement. I had not managed to talk to any Native Americans yet and we were leaving Santa Fe that day. I told the o-m, who did not share my need, I'd join him in a little while.

At the end of the street an artisan with a gentle open face had rows of turquoise jewellery laid out on a blanket on the ground. I asked her where the turquoise came from. She told me it came from Arizona, another often-arid state that was actually part of New Mexico when it was under

Mexican rule. Her home was Santo Domingo Pueblo, forty kilometres south of Santa Fe. She would cut and thread the pieces, using three strands of nylon to make the necklace strings. How long did it take? Cutting the pieces was labour intensive, she said, but she didn't clock the hours. Once a week her son dropped her off in Santa Fe to sell it. She had had a slow day.

It sounds so little but through this conversation I was able to picture the turquoise being mined in Arizona and transported to the pueblo. I imagined the pueblo and the painstaking care taken with the cutting of the stones. The sense of a human being at one with the stone as it was cut. The recklessness with the hours. Patience and courtesy on the pavement. Her son coming to pick her up, asking how her day had gone. Later on, I would google Santo Domingo Pueblo and discover its long history of mining and sourcing turquoise and its fine reputation for quality craftsmanship through recorded history.

I tried on a necklace. It was a string of threaded oval beads, aquamarine with brown veins, with a price tag of US$75. I had $80 but the trader didn't have the right change so I handed her $60, saying I'd go to an ATM to get change. I expected her to ask me to leave the necklace with her while I was away, but she merely said, 'It's nearly packing-up time but I will wait for you.' Trusting me.

After taking a few steps down the road I couldn't go on. Went back and handed her the $20. Her trust that the world was still a place where people could be honest with one another expanded my world into something more generous and genuinely interactive.

I took a photo of the jewellery and would have included her in it, but she expressed a strong distaste for that. At the time I didn't know about that cultural belief that such an image could rob a person of her power; I thought she was just shy. For a moment, like the congenital colonial I am, I considered including her secretly. Instead I asked her name. Rose. A gift equal to a photograph. By the time I reached the museum it was just on closing time, so I missed seeing the paintings. The o-m said they were glorious.

That evening as we walked to the station for our train, a blood-red sunset suffused the sky. In the foreground was the cathedral, with its curtain of mountains behind. The o-m said that O'Keeffe had rendered such colours in her landscapes of New Mexico. Whenever I recall Santa Fe, I see the cathedral and the mountains. In my memory, the cathedral is no longer Archbishop Lamy's; it belongs to the sunset and Santa Fe.

9
Willa Cather in Disputed Territory

9

Willa Cather in Disputed Territory

Many months would elapse before I came back to the question of Padre Martinez and his eponymous character in Cather's novel. Also, the question of whether Father Latour was an accurate representation of Archbishop Lamy. I would be home and nearly halfway through writing this book before the roulette dice made the matter unavoidable. By then *Death Comes for the Archbishop* had become for me, as for thousands if not millions of Americans, part of the mythology of frontier America. Cather presented her character, Father Latour, as representative of a period of history, a period that began with the buffalo and ended with railway trains steaming into Santa Fe. Through the eyes of this character, and of his creator too, I saw the history of New Mexico unfold with hope and optimism.

For most of the novel, Cather is on firm ground, both in her soaring prose and her historical allusions. She claimed that the novel followed very closely the real story of the first archbishop of Santa Fe and that from her reading of letters the two priests wrote home to their families; she could vouch for how they had reacted to their new environment.

Father Latour arrives in a land recently annexed by the United States. Its people are mainly Mexican and Native Americans. He finds that, as a result of determined evangelism, both races number many Catholics, but often they have to fend for themselves for long periods. No wonder, for it is a vast territory to cover in the course of episcopal duties and the terrain is extremely harsh. As Father Latour travels on his mule through the vast country, he comes to know its particular energy well. He is deeply affected by the vast cracks and fissures in the ground around him, the colours of the sparse vegetation and by the shape of things, for instance the way that giant rock rises starkly from a surrounding flatness. He learns to use Spanish words such as mesa, arroyo, canyon. As he comes to know the land, through journeys that sometimes take months to complete, he develops a sense of spiritual connection.

From Mexican friends Father Latour hears stories of the Spanish fathers, including the tragic interaction with the Acoma people, but he also hears stories of gentler and wiser priests. From Indian friends, he learns of their ways and beliefs, both Pueblo and nomad, and realises there are things in their culture he will never understand, though he respects them.

He loves to see how people of many different cultures and religions have intertwined to become the entity of New Mexico. He sees this embodied in the Angelus bell in Santa Fe, whose history goes all the way back to the Moors. Of Spanish provenance, it was transported from Mexico, but the silver was originally Moorish. His dream is for New Mexico to become a united Great Diocese. He believes a

Catholic church that transcends nationality and ethnicity could achieve this.

Father Latour wishes that Padre Martinez could have used his undoubted talents more constructively. He exemplifies priests of the old school who stand in the way of such unity and who have strayed far from the Ten Commandments. Although the Padre is very popular, Father Latour has heard stories of his lechery and debauchery, of having fathered children throughout his jurisdiction. People even say it was Martinez who instigated the Taos Revolt in 1847 — that when the rebels were arrested, he promised to help them if they would deed him their land. They did so but were executed anyway. Martinez proceeded to cultivate their farms and was soon the wealthiest man in the parish. The only thing to be done with him, from Latour's point of view, is excommunication, which he expedites as soon as possible.

The deep affection held by Father Latour for his devoted assistant, Father Joseph Vaillant, helps them both survive their tough calling. Their differences are mostly complementary and they hold the greatest respect for one another. Father Latour is gifted in reconciling differences that in less skilled hands might cause bitterness and even estrangement. For instance, the question of whether or not something is a miracle. Father Joseph likes his miracles immediate and spectacular, matters of concrete signs, such as unseasonal roses growing among rocks. Father Latour believes miracles can be understood as the way that perceptions are trans- formed by profound love. Such love enables us to see and hear what is truly around us all the time.

Father Latour is also able to find sustenance and spiritual strength from people of other cultures. A young Mexican woman, Magdalena, held captive by her evil husband, regains strength and beauty when she is freed to go and live with the Loreto Sisters. A Mexican slave woman, Sada, whose owners forbad her to go to church, inspires Latour with her unquestioning faith at a time when his own was faltering. A Navajo man, Eusabio, embodies the Indian way of passing through a country without having any desire to master it. Cather emphasises this essential cultural difference.

She describes how Father Latour, in dedicating his life to the time and place in which he finds himself, slowly becomes something not French, not Mexican or Indian or Anglo but — American. If prevented from carrying out a project immediately, he waits patiently for the universal force that he calls God to work its will. He builds his cathedral, a fusion of European architecture with American stone and setting. He cultivates his garden and makes sure that the priests he brings over from France know how to grow fruit trees, vegetables and flowers, not by exacting unfair contributions from native peoples as Baltazar had done, but by the work of their own hands.

These qualities are in opposition to those generally accepted to pertain to the real archbishop. Unlike Father Latour, Archbishop Lamy was a man of his times. He was dismissive of native Santo art, unable to understand the deep social and religious needs served by the Penitente Brotherhood and simply wrong in his estimation and treatment of Padre Martinez.

After Mexico became independent in 1821, the Franciscans went back to Spain, leaving a religious vacuum. Now that native New Mexicans were allowed to become pastors, Padre Martinez trained some of them in Durango, Mexico. The Penitente Brotherhood offered a partial substitute for churches without an ordained priest, but many condemned their practices of self-flagellation. Though a few American Protestant missionaries came to Santa Fe, what they had to offer was generally too plain and sombre to have much appeal for a people who loved ritual, spectacle and deep symbolism.

Then in 1851 Father Lamy was appointed bishop-designate for New Mexico. He came from Clermont-Ferrand in France, an area known for its Catholic zeal, and had been trained in a seminary famed for its doctrinal rigour. He was scathing about the Penitentes and saw great danger in the few American Protestant missionaries who made it to New Mexico. He spared nothing in trying to prevent them from establishing their 'errors' in New Mexico. Critical of New Mexican clergy, he ceaselessly promoted French priests to replace them, and in 1864 he claimed that he personally was responsible for twenty-one missionaries who had come from the diocese of Clermont-Ferrand.

In the transition from Mexican to US rule, the question of what it meant to be American was much discussed. Definitely it entailed separation of church and state, a concept foreign to New Mexico's Spanish and Mexican heritage. It also meant accepting religious diversity in place of monolithic Catholicism. Lamy found this deeply threatening. He remained staunchly anti-Protestant, virulent in his opposition to Protestant-run schools even if it meant no schools at all. This is a far cry from Father Latour, who loved to see how people of many different cultures and religions had intertwined to become the entity of New Mexico. *He* became American in the most positive, inclusive sense of the word. This was how many Americans wanted to see themselves and may partly account for the novel's popularity.

However, although the novel is one of acceptance and reconciliation, it works against itself because of the way Cather represents Padre Martinez. It is now generally agreed that there is no historical evidence for the behaviour Cather lays at the padre's door, especially the claim that Martinez organised the Taos Revolt. He did protest the executions, believing they unfairly punished men who were only defending their land and way of life. Caring passionately about education, he established a college for students of both sexes and published religious and political pieces at his own expense. He became New Mexico's most significant educator in the nineteenth century and one of its important publishers. He fought for many years against the system of tithing which impoverished his parishioners. He withheld judgement against the Penitente Brotherhood, understanding that it emerged in response to the scarcity of priests. He was open and friendly to Christian missionaries of other denominations.

It's possible that Father Martinez did father a number of children in his jurisdiction — there were certainly some he took particular responsibility for and treated as his family. On the other hand the charge may have arisen from his habit of referring to his 'children' in the sense that he was their spiritual father. There is no evidence that he had the yellow eyes and long yellow teeth of Cather's fictional rendition.

One reason for Cather's version of the padre may be that she needed a character who was powerful and bad, someone to set in opposition to the saintly figure of the Archbishop. But why did Cather retain the real name of her padre while granting Lamy and his assistant Joseph Machebeuf fictional disguise? She wrote somewhere that the novel could not be at the same time a form of imaginative art and a vivid and brilliant form of journalism. In her mind there was no contest — the imaginative art was all-important. Perhaps this felt like a licence to represent as art dictated.

Why did Cather choose such different interpretations of the characters of these men? I'm inclined to think the reason had to with the profoundness of her connection with her material. When she heard the story of the two priests from France, she was inspired with an unstoppable passion to write it. In letters written after the novel's completion, she often referred to 'my Archbishop' as if she had a real working relationship with him. She chose for her next project something frivolous and sentimental, a reaction she regarded as a natural result of her year of 'celibacy with the Archbishop'.

She loved France. As a teenager she began to read novels in French and for many years preferred French writers to contemporary English ones. She found them more direct and sincere, with a wider range of interest. On a train ride through France she had had an epiphany. She saw a reaper she recognised as an American brand and immediately saw in her mind's eye a girl sitting on it, between her father's feet. This was her inspiration for *O Pioneers!* and marked the beginning of her mature career. The culture, literature, language, art and cuisine all excited her and she believed that the French love of order and discipline was what inspired the measured lives of Fathers Latour and Vaillant, lives that reminded her of a work of art. For Cather there was no higher praise.

The inspiration she experienced from learning the story of Joseph Machebeuf combined with her visiting Santa Fe and seeing there a French cathedral must have offered her the stuff of epic. This magic linkage of her beloved France and a place (this time, New Mexico) provided the tinder to set *the Archbishop* in motion. A few bare facts became, through Cather's process of fictionalising them, a source of enduring fulfilment. She was able to step back from the alienation she felt from her own time and space, the years after World War I that she described as a time 'the world broke in two', and render the world as it was in an era when moral values still felt meaningful and important. She wrote of the glorious year she had, working in a new form without solid drama, that brought her deep content.

Her sense of profound transformation may have blinded her to the effect on Hispanic readers of her slurs against the real Padre Martinez. They had not had an easy time transitioning from Spanish-Mexican to Mexican-American identity and their status among white Americans was always precarious. Many of them were alienated by Cather's version of Padre Martinez, which for many decades was accepted as the true one.

Cather's version of Father Martinez may be partly attributable to her sources, including the Machebeuf biography which may have been biased against Martinez. And she was of her times in presenting the past through one person's part in it, thus aligning herself with Thomas Carlyle's widely accepted Great Man theory of history. However, Father Latour's final assessment was that in fact it was Father Vaillant who had accomplished more.

There was one more question I wanted to explore. It puzzled me that the protagonist/antagonist tension persists throughout the novel, even though the padre dies relatively early on. As I read more about the real Padre Martinez, I was astonished by Patricia Clark Smith's claim that Cather based the structure of her novel upon Homer's *Odyssey*. I have never really understood the fascination with the *Odyssey* and at first I was disinclined to believe in a connection with *the Archbishop*, but as I read Smith's essay and checked out similarities and echoes between Odysseus's adventures and incidents in the novel, I concluded it was indisputable. Martinez himself bears a resemblance to the sorceress Circe, who takes advantage of people's simplicity before turning them into swine, and whose magnetism is such that Odysseus, after outwitting her, stayed on day after day until a whole year had passed. Like Circe, Cather's Martinez is charismatic and, like Circe, Martinez exploits people's simplicity before turning them into swine — as represented in *the Archbishop* by the Padre's very swinish theology student, Trinidad.

Resonances with the *Odyssey* dwindle and disappear as Cather's characters express increasing appreciation for the complexities of colonisation and unease about its drawbacks. Father Latour becomes acutely aware of Native American reluctance to master nature. He begins to see the great industrial expansion instigated by the colonisers has fostered a culture in which trickery and deceit are inseparable from honourable ambition. Such progress receives its comeuppance in devastating reverses. Father Latour, who has learned to love the fragrances of hot sun, sagebrush and sweet clover that waft in through his windows, fears they may be lost as civilisation progresses. For the sake of the fragrances he loves, he returns to New Mexico to die.

In the end I think Father Latour's dawning understanding of the complex consequences of colonisation is what saves the novel from becoming dated. Influential present-day readers are attempting to give Father Martinez a fairer assessment and if they can show that the pain inflicted on Hispanos was never Cather's intention, then the novel can become for them too a way of seeing the past that offers hope for reconciliation between the races. As Professor Bette Weidman pointed out in a collection of essays about Padre Martinez, Willa Cather would have hated for her novel to undermine a reader's self-image or make them discount the importance of their father figures.[31]

The great region where Cather is *not* in disputed territory is that of the land itself. That territory comes through so vividly it is like a living character. In her hands inanimate things like hills come alive, pushing and elbowing each other aside, while plants resemble a colony of lizards, transfixed by fear. Even the vegetation quakes before the immense emptiness of its surroundings.

Before my visit to New Mexico, my reading of *Death Comes for the Archbishop* made me feel as though I knew the land already. After the visit when I reread it, the impression became indelible. In my mind's eye I see the old route from

Taos to Santa Fe, studded with ravines that a priest's carriage could roll down, ravines that only the bravest or most foolish would navigate and then only with help of axe and shovel. I am conscious of a road that went before, that gives the current road solidity and meaning. It gives New Mexico the substance of history, of people who went before, of a different kind of interaction between land and people. Travelling through these regions of Willa Cather's imagination, I see a place where Native Americans and Mexicans were *the* people, not adjuncts to those who came later.

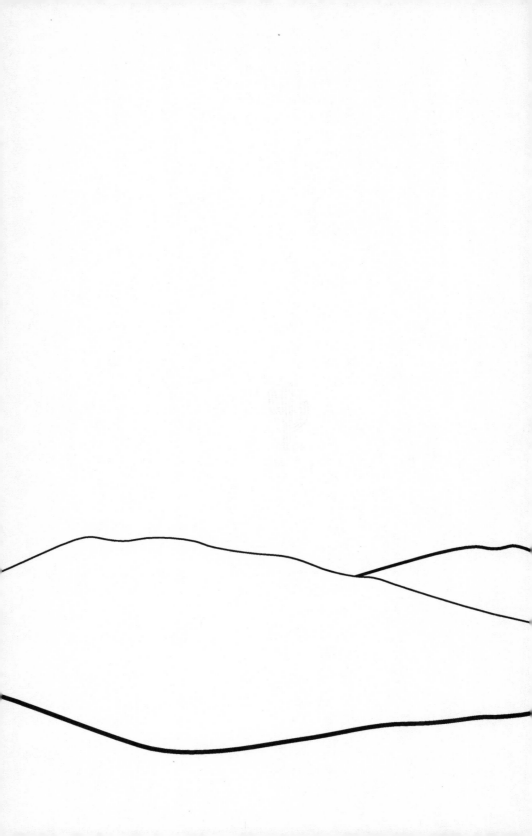

10

Red Hills and Black Mesa with Georgia O'Keeffe

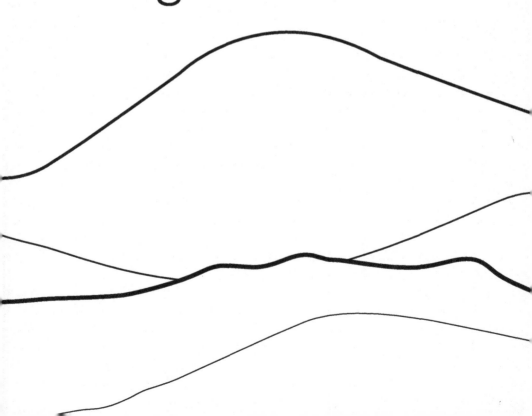

One of the guest rooms in the Big House was named Georgia O'Keeffe. Each time I passed that sign, my imagination summoned images of flowers painted so close up that they brimmed with erotic intensity. After I came home I discovered it was not flowers O'Keeffe was revered for in the Southwest but her artistic embodiment of New Mexico. A book of colour plates of her work revealed how she had managed to capture the colours and monumental geology of the high desert. In New Mexico I had been struck by the grandness, vastness and emptiness, but until I saw these paintings I hadn't connected emotionally.

I learned later that her influence was so great that after her death Americans took to referring to New Mexico as O'Keeffe country. It wasn't fair on Native Americans and Hispanos whose people had lived there for centuries, but it wasn't fair on O'Keeffe either. Her attitude was never one of cultural appropriation. However, the term was also and more fairly used to refer to the region around Abiquiu where she lived for many years and where she painted the majority of her landscapes.

The name on the door suggested that, like other artists in search of greater freedom and creativity, O'Keeffe too had been drawn into Mabel's circle. When the dice came to a halt before the sign, I set out to uncover how the association came about and found that it began with O'Keeffe seeking Mabel's help.

As a young woman O'Keeffe came to live in New York after the influential photographer and art dealer Alfred Stieglitz saw some of her charcoal drawings and was so impressed he exhibited them at his gallery, 291. When O'Keeffe came to 291 to complain that he hadn't asked her permission, they found themselves drawn to one another. Stieglitz continued to promote and exhibit her work and they became intensely involved on a personal level although Stieglitz was married at the time and twenty-three years older than O'Keeffe. They married in 1924.

Stieglitz was a dedicated advocate for American modern art. He was also on a mission to help people understand photography as an art form. After O'Keeffe came to live in New York, he found a new focus of interest. Over the next seven years he photographed her obsessively, often in the nude. Meanwhile, O'Keeffe was trying to make space in the male world of art for her own iconoclastic vision. Skyscrapers were changing the skyline and male artists were claiming the new subject matter for themselves. O'Keeffe painted her own skyscrapers – seen as from below, like a person looking up at the intimidating, human-dwarfing structures. She also began painting flowers and worked out a new way of drawing that focussed attention on them by making them 'big like the huge buildings going up'. As she said,

— nobody sees a flower — really — it is so small — we haven't time — and to see takes time, like to have a friend takes time... So I said to myself — I'll paint what I see — what the flower is to me but I'll paint it big and they will be surprised into taking time to look at it — I will make even busy New-Yorkers take time to see what I see of flowers.[32]

What the men saw — and commented on in their scholarly, authoritative way — was vaginas writ large, an intention O'Keeffe denied. They claimed that many of her paintings were an outlet for sexual frustration. This, combined with the publicity surrounding her husband's hundreds of photographs of her nude body, overshadowed her mastery of form and colour. O'Keeffe found herself in a straitjacket so she requested help from Mabel, whom she admired,

I thought you could write something about me that the men can't — What I want written — I do not know — I have no definite idea of what it should be — but a woman who has lived many things and who sees lines and colors as an expression of living — might say something that a man can't — I feel there is something unexplored about woman that only a woman can explore. Men have done all they can do about it. Does that mean anything to you — or doesn't it?[33]

Mabel came to see Georgia's 1925 show, but her response put her in a quandary. Deeply confused about her own sexuality, she saw the show as a 'filthy spectacle of frustration'.[34] She wrote an essay about it, which she never published. Despite her visceral reaction, she became friends with Georgia and invited her to Taos. She tried several times without success but by 1929 Georgia was at a low ebb with both her art and her marriage to Stieglitz. They loved one another passionately with a commitment that would endure until his death, but their agreement on an open marriage complicated their relationship.

When Stieglitz and a young volunteer at the gallery, Dorothy Norman, became lovers, O'Keeffe fell into depression. Her friend, painter Rebecca Salsbury James, had previously sung Mabel's praises as a host and told Georgia she would 'do some great things' if she came. And Brett, who was in New York that year, spoke enthusiastically about Taos. Stieglitz wasn't well enough to travel, so Georgia went with Rebecca.

They stayed that summer in the Pink House, a guesthouse alive with artistic resonance. Willa Cather had stayed there a few years earlier and Lawrence, Frieda and Brett had spent many happy hours decorating it for Mabel. On the front door Georgia would have found Lawrence's phoenix rising from the flames and, on the outside bathroom door, his huge painted sunflower. Mabel gave her a studio and, surrounded by vast dramatic landforms and a magical clarity of light, she found her creativity again.

There were other photographers and artists at the Big House that summer seeking a change that would expand their artistic perceptions. Photographer Ansel Adams and his wife Virginia Best had been there since March. Adams was working on a book on Taos Pueblo in collaboration with Mary Austin and she had sent them to Mabel's. With Tony's help, Ansel obtained full access to take photos at the pueblo. He and Georgia loved the adobe buildings and the uncompromising shadows their planes created in the burning sun. They saw in the adobe, and in its connection with the earth, a kind of spirituality. This prompted Ansel from then on to build his photos from a starting point of light and form. He and Georgia became lifelong friends.

Georgia and Rebecca persuaded Mabel to invite another artist from the Stieglitz Circle. This was the watercolourist John Marin. He had been looking for a new landscape and in Taos he learned to capture movement as he never had before, by observing how the clouds created light and shadow on earth. After several weeks of just looking, he suddenly produced a series of watercolours which O'Keeffe and others agreed placed him in the first rank of American artists.

Ansel found Marin fascinating and his paintings revelatory, but it was his discussions with Rebecca's husband Paul Strand the following summer that were truly transformational. Ansel called Strand the mentor whose work 'hit him like Saul's vision on the road to Damascus'.[35] He dropped his concert pianist ambitions and gave up trying to simulate painting with his photographs.

Georgia wrote that she was having such a wonderful time that she didn't care if Europe fell off the map, and the energy of her fellow travellers seemed to agree with her, 'One perfect day after another — everyone going like mad after something.'[36]

Mabel watched her transformation. Initially, Georgia appeared 'demure as a nun, in black, with a shadowed face and quiet, resigned hands',[37] but that didn't last long. Mabel noticed that Georgia's eyes were deepening and her voice escaping her control, 'it rose in flooding ecstasies; unbelieved excitements thrilled her through and through, and feelings that had slept beside her old man awakened and reminded her she was alive and disinterred'.

Mabel was less thrilled when she realised that O'Keeffe's transformation had a lot to do with Tony. Soon after her arrival Georgia painted *After a Walk Back of Mabel's*, a large picture which Mabel read as a painting of her husband. In the apparent rock forms she saw the sweep of his vermilion blanket against a burning blue sky, 'an enormous dark, strong, bulking shape as big as a world, against which seemed to crouch a small, weak, paler form'. The paler form, Mabel was sure, represented Georgia, an unsure Georgia crying the cry of the unborn. The figure was so expressive that another guest remarked on it, 'How the little one is howling!' And Mabel never forgot

Georgia's agonised reply, 'Oh! Is it *howling*?'[38]

The last thing Mabel wanted was a repeat of what had happened the previous winter when Tony had had an affair with another friend of theirs, Marion Shevky. When questioned, Tony acknowledged he couldn't deny he loved Marion; he could only say she didn't have Mabel's place and that he couldn't live or love anyone if he didn't have her. Mabel remembered that she too made 'occasional detours'.

Such side-trips were common in her circles. There was a considerable degree of openness about what was happening and spouses coped as best they could. Mabel told Georgia about Tony's affair, but contrary to her hopes, the information only added to her new guest's fascination. Mabel was dismayed,

> 'She leapt with excitement and said we could change it.
> Instead of putting her off and making her feel he was
> completely occupied, it gave her an excuse to be attentive
> to him! She was able to feel she was doing it to help me,
> and she applied herself . . . In fact, her unconscious
> wish completely defeated my effort to get her thoughts
> off him!'[39]

Mabel confided to Ansel, during a spell at a sanatorium, that she suspected an affair between Georgia and Tony. She told him how she was struggling with her reaction, 'I *love* her and feel like being generous but Oh dear! This ego! . . . All the women in the place like Tony! . . . Maybe that was my mission when I married Tony! To provide a bridge between Indians & white people! . . . That's a fine mission for a selfish egotistic woman to find herself involved in!'[40]

A month or so after Georgia's arrival, Mabel had to go to Buffalo, over 3000 kilometres away, for a radical hysterectomy. While she was away, Tony took Georgia into Navajo country and talked about the land and culture.

Mabel understood from Georgia's letters how much Tony meant to her, 'she was exalted with joy and vitality and her happiness spread over the pages'.[41] Tony could not write to Mabel in English, so Georgia read out her letters and acted as his scribe. She tried to allay Mabel's suspicions,

> 'Right now as I come fresh from six days spent mostly with your Tony — I want to tell you that next to my Stieglitz I have found nothing finer than your Tony . . . if Tony doesn't love you — according to my notion — then nobody ever will . . . I have rarely seen something in two people . . . as I feel it between you and your Tony and I feel you have got to let him live and *be* his way — however much it might hurt you . . . Even if he goes out and sleeps with someone else it is a little thing — oh dear this sounds like twaddle but I love something that I feel together in you — and when I see such things being destroyed — it just makes me not want to live.'[42]

Mabel was deeply unhappy and Georgia's attempts at reassurance did not help. Georgia left soon after she returned from Buffalo and the following summer when Georgia returned, Mabel told her to leave Tony alone. After that the two women kept their distance. Georgia, however, could not keep her distance from the Southwest, which had claimed her heart forever.

During her two summers in Taos, O'Keeffe produced eighteen new works, which Stieglitz showed at his new gallery, An American Place, giving her at least one major exhibition each year. One of the works was of the ponderosa pine at the ranch where Lawrence had lived. He used to sit and write on a bench underneath it and of all the things he later missed about New Mexico, it was this tree that called to him. O'Keeffe liked to lie down on the bench so that the tree looked as though it was standing on its head. She used that exact perspective for her famous painting *The Lawrence Tree*.

In another work she placed a Penitente cross in front of Taos mountain, a positioning that reminds the viewer of Christianity's far-reaching effect upon the pre-existing beliefs of the Native Americans. The cross looks like an attempt to blot out everything behind it, but the sacred mountain radiates its own ineradicable power.

Her personal life was turbulent. Stieglitz's continuing affair with Dorothy Norman affected her profoundly and that distress was compounded by continuing grief over her brother's death at the Western Front. In 1934 she returned to New Mexico and discovered an adobe house in a location seemingly made for her. She was able to rent this property, Rancho de los Burros, which was on Ghost Ranch about sixty kilometres southwest of Taos and just north of the village of Abiquiu.

The landscape around the ranch featured Cerro Pedernal, a flat-topped mountain that Georgia claimed God would give to her if she painted it enough. She revelled in the monumental rock forms with their almost surreal colours and the light that was so different from anything she had experienced outside New Mexico. Each year she returned until in 1940 she bought the house.

She became friendly or, in her words, intimate, with Dorothy Brett. Since Lawrence's death, Brett's art had flowered as New Mexico allowed her true artistic self to emerge. In that the two were kindred spirits, though O'Keeffe found Brett's brand of eccentricity, coupled with her increasing deafness, hard to handle and after a while she preferred more distance.

She continued to paint pictures of flowers, especially those discounted by others, such as jimsonweed, a species of datura naturalised in the Southwest. In 1932 she painted *Jimson Weed/White Flower No 1*, which later hung in the White House for six years at the request of Laura Bush, and in 1936 when commissioned by Elizabeth Arden she painted *Jimson Weed*, a composition of four of the pinwheel-shaped flower heads. The largest of her flower paintings, an imposing 180 x 212 centimetres, it hung in the exercise room of the new Arden Sport Salon in New York, encouraging patrons to stretch and unfurl like the flowers. It currently hangs in the Indianapolis Museum of Art.

Gradually she became interested in the bleached bones she found in the desert. Ghost Ranch itself had been a working cattle ranch until it fell victim to the Dust Bowl years, immortalised in John Steinbeck's *Grapes of Wrath*, that left so many animal skeletons in its wake. O'Keeffe shipped some of the bones to New York where she spent winter months gradually rendering them into semi-abstract paintings.

Georgia loved to travel about. After the confinements of Manhattan and the gender-based assessments of her work, she revelled in this new-found freedom. On foot, by horse, car, train or plane, all were a delight. Soon after her arrival, she bought a Model A Ford and fitted it out for excursions into the wilderness.

On one of her early trips she discovered a stretch of 'badlands' about 240 kilometres northwest of Ghost Ranch. Like other badlands it had been formed by a process of deposition followed by erosion. Over millions of years, these layers of mineral material had accumulated. Once they solidified, the softer sedimentary rocks and soils were eroded by wind and water until canyons, ravines, gullies and mesas were formed. As O'Keeffe approached these badlands the repeated formations of grey hills rising from almost white sand reminded her of elephants. To O'Keeffe this became the 'Black Place' and, in the 1940s, a favourite haunt for camping trips. It inspired a new kind of abstraction in her work and a new level of productivity. In 1944 and 1945 she produced six completed canvases, a large pastel and at least nine pencil sketches.

The more I look at her pictures, the more deeply they affect me. It's the hills especially, her series featuring red hills, black mesa, grey hills, purple hills, white cliffs and beautiful, startling yellow hills, all suffused with the unearthly New Mexican light that is so powerfully and uniquely free of moisture. There's something in the way she simplifies forms, intensifies colours, fogs the distinction between two- and three-dimensional effects. She reduces rough surfaces to smooth, flattened planes and eliminates most of the trees but the effect is paradoxical. By making objects seem flat and compressed in space, she achieves something riveting to the eye, something that redefines what she has seen and makes us see it that way too.

There is, as in her flower paintings, some sexual charge, revealed in these paintings as a kind of universal, animating force far bigger and more potent than sexuality, but it makes me catch my breath when it is exposed for all to see.

Though she eschews any obvious human presence, by abstracting from the real she inserts the human: the human eye, human sensibility – the human need for rhythm, intensity, movement, animation. The landscape is made to relate to human consciousness, giving her art the power to change us by changing our perception of what we see. I want to go back to see the originals and also the actual hills she painted, to learn to see and feel them as she did. I am enriched, enlarged, made more substantial by her creation.

Isolated though her home was, it could not insulate her from the effects of hubris driven by fear. Los Alamos was only fifty kilometres away and Georgia was in residence as the intensive laboratory experiments of the Manhattan Project pushed forward. The atomic scientists began coming to the ranch on a weekend basis. They came under assumed names and everything about their work was top secret. No one mentioned Trinity, the code name for the world's impending first nuclear test. Georgia was usually disinclined to fraternise with other guests so probably spent little time with them.[43]

When the test was detonated, sudden winds whipped the desert sands against buildings and the land shook as if in an earthquake. The physicist Ernest Lawrence described how the sky went from darkness to brilliant sunshine in an instant.

What did O'Keeffe think about all this? No mention in letters to her husband, no comment through her art – or was there? For years after the event, the government did not allow photographs to circulate, yet *Red with Yellow*, a painting in her Pelvis Series, produced in the summer of 1945, bears an uncanny resemblance in its colour and feeling to the only colour photograph that was taken. The Pelvis Series were paintings that drew inspiration from a cow's pelvis, which were among the many bones O'Keeffe found in the desert. Characteristically, she zeroed in on the pelvis, using the hole in the bone as a way of viewing the sky beyond. Blues and whites were favourite colours, 'The pelvis bone is most beautiful against the blue, that blue that will always be there as it is now, after all man's destruction is finished.'[44]

But in *Red with Yellow* the hole is filled with brilliant yellow surrounded by a red light, giving the effect of sunrise or sunset. This painting became one of the most famous of the series. It could have been inspired by no more than a bone with a hole in it, but it is possible to see in it a record of that explosion.

The following year, Stieglitz had a stroke. Georgia flew to New York but he died soon afterwards. Their relationship had endured for thirty years and had brought sustained nourishment and inspiration to both. Georgia put enormous effort into sorting his affairs and finding good homes for his artworks. After three years she was at last ready to return to New Mexico where she then settled permanently.

Despite having bought her home on Ghost Ranch, she

proceeded to buy another property just nineteen kilometres away in Abiquiu. This was no sudden decision. Years earlier, she had fallen in love with a door. She used to climb over the outer wall of the ruined hacienda that contained it just to see this double door with tile stepping stones in front of it, which opened onto an interior courtyard. Something about the door spoke to Georgia, who subsequently painted it many times, but it took ten years before the owners allowed her to buy the property.

The house was a combination of many styles and historical periods. It included nineteen interior doors of different heights and composition and sixteen exterior doors opening onto gardens and the interior courtyard. These helped retain its historic character, though Georgia made many changes and was so tired of the upkeep required for adobe that she coated the outside walls with cement stucco.

The atomic bomb project impeded progress when she had to compete for nails and other building materials. Instead of planking she had to get raw wood off the mountain. After the Soviet Union tested its first hydrogen bomb in 1953, she built a bomb shelter a few feet from her studio and added *The Effects of Atomic Weapons*, published by the Los Alamos scientific laboratory, to her library. But if she was deeply affected by the destructive potential developing around her, I found no evidence to prove it.

Why did Georgia want this house so much? She felt a profound need for a garden and had found it impossible to grow things she wanted at Ghost Ranch. Yet she loved the vastness and grandeur of its surroundings far too much to abandon it. At Abiquiu she was able to create a garden full of meaning, a garden that expressed her deepest self and her sense of place and that at the same time connected her with a vast spiritual landscape — the Chama River Valley with its astonishing array of colours in sedimentary rocks formed nearly a million years ago.

Georgia in fact cultivated several gardens — a walled vegetable garden, a garden for cut flowers, an orchard and interior patios each nurturing one or two plants. The house and garden provided the perfect grounding for her new life without Stieglitz. She lived at both properties, dividing her time between the two until, eventually, failing eyesight forced her to leave Abiquiu for Santa Fe, where she died in 1986 at the age of ninety-eight.

After her death her reputation continued to grow and in 1997 the Georgia O'Keeffe Museum was opened in Santa Fe. Her 1932 painting of jimsonweed was donated to the museum, which later sold it. In 2014 it sold again to Walmart heiress Alice Walton for $44.4 million, the highest price for a work of art by a female artist ever sold at auction.

We have to make the gender distinction — though the sum was huge for a woman, the work of male artists could dwarf it. A painting by Jackson Pollock sold for $140 million in 2006; one painting from Cézanne's *The Card Players* series was bought for $259 million in 2011. In an article for the *Guardian*, Jonathan Jones speculated that the reason there were no acknowledged great female artists was because of men like him. Art criticism, he wrote, is a macho trade and the views expressed are mainly those of male critics. Jones says that passion for an artist involves a sense of deep identification and it's easier for a man to identify more deeply with, for instance, Pollock's 'rangy cowboy grandeur' than O'Keeffe's 'sensual ranchhouse splendour'.[45] So let's not get complacent.

11

An Offer
of Beauty from
Millicent Rogers

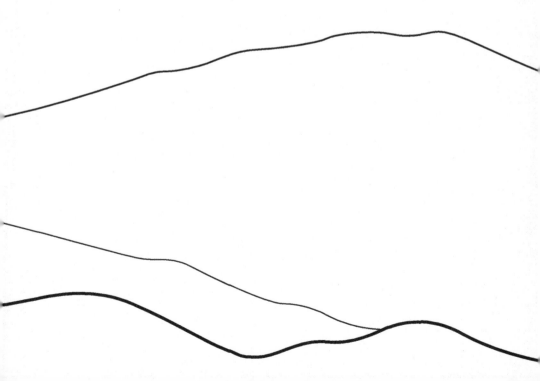

11

An Offer
of Beauty from
Millicent Rogers

My last throw at the roulette table before leaving Taos calls up Millicent Rogers, the person whose collection of artefacts of the Southwest formed the basis of the Millicent Rogers Museum.

I was lucky to be taken there by Sam, Rebecca and Sharon, the Americans I met on my first night at the Big House. Passing from one object to another, I realised I would find every object beautiful and began to experience a peculiar sense of connection with the mind that had gathered all these objects together. I had never experienced a stronger statement about the value of beauty. Afterwards Sam and I bought copies of a letter Millicent had written to her son Paul not long before her death. We were moved by the sentiment that began, 'Suddenly passing Taos Mountain I felt that I was part of the Earth'. Something much deeper here was going on than an impossibly rich heiress buying whatever she felt like to impress others and make herself feel less mortal.

Millicent was neither artist nor writer, but her life was a creative celebration of beauty, beginning with her own, which she tended as reverentially as the other beautiful things in her life. Mabel, who knew her many years later, referred to Millicent's brand of creativity in her unpublished memoir, 'The Statue of Liberty',

> Her make-up was never too obvious or high coloured, but all of her yellowed skin was daily covered with the most delicate shades in shadows, her eyes enlarged and her mouth fabricated out of nothing. There was no basis for what she created, nothing underneath; it was all made new every day.[46]

The immense fortune built up by her tycoon grandfather in Standard Oil enabled her to pursue every dream money could buy. She showered her houses with love in the only way she knew — by turning them into exquisitely beautiful objects brimming with beautiful things. In the Austrian Alps she and her second husband, Arturo Peralta-Ramos, built a chalet that Millicent honoured with an ingenious mix of Biedermeier antiques, papier-mâché chairs, needlework carpets and Austrian porcelain stoves. Back in the States with her third husband, Ronald Balcom, she renovated an historic house in Virginia in accordance with its eighteenth-century British grandeur.

Inside, her Biedermeier furniture and collection of European art found an inspired fit with striped wallpaper and beaded needlepoint cushions on a velvet sofa. On this country estate, which had hosted every US president since the Civil War, Millicent entertained in lavish American style. The slave quarters became guesthouses and she converted the overseer's office into a music library.

Her final house was in Taos. Turtle Walk, as she called it for its cluster of small turtle-shaped rooms, was an old adobe house weighed down by its twenty-two truckloads of insulating dirt on the roof. She mended it with her customary elan, keeping the traditional vigas but rendering them dark blue, while she painted the walls deep Indian-red and yellow. Above all, she changed the positioning of doors and windows until the effect pleased her. She even moved the entire master bedroom by fifteen centimetres so that she could see Taos Mountain from her bed.

In Europe she had acquired paintings by Monet, Cézanne and Toulouse-Lautrec, while in Taos she accumulated several thousand pieces of Navajo, Zuni and Hopi silverwork and jewellery, Navajo and Hispanic textiles, Pueblo pottery and basketry of the Western Apache tribes.

She also designed clothes that aligned her body with the spirit of her homes. In her Austrian chalet, she wore Tyrolean peasant dresses; she graced the Virginian mansion in puffed sleeves and wide ankle-length skirts complete with tassels and beads that chimed with her Biedermeier furniture. As for Turtle Walk, the Pueblo influence came through in squaw skirts and short waisted jackets trimmed with silver Navajo buttons and butterflies. Fashion and style magazines such as *Vogue* and *Harper's Bazaar* loved it all.

For most of her life, bodily adornment was her greatest passion and she stinted nothing in achieving the look she wanted. She scarcely had to make choices — sometimes she ordered bales of shirts at a time — but she had an eye for style. She was able to take elements of current fashion and combine them with rough or ethnic elements in a way that not only expressed her own beauty but set off fashion trends. The Tyrolean dress for instance. When the fashion moguls decreed that every woman of style would wear a beret that winter, Millicent wore a Tyrolean hat. When she wore dirndls (a traditional Austrian dress), Wallis Simpson commissioned her designers to make Tyrolean outfits for her honeymoon.

She even modelled a ski jacket after one she had seen on an Italian truck driver. To the truckie's flamboyant orange lining she added a red-fox collar. She was often photographed in fashion magazines, and commercial designers took her vision into account when creating theirs. In Paris they thought she was the first American woman with any style.

Plagued by a weak heart, the result of rheumatic fever as a child, Millicent made her precarious health work for her. During periods of hospitalisation, she learned languages and drawing, deepened her appreciation of music and translated Rilke for fun. She understood that disability could be turned to advantage if she could find positive aspects in it and adapt to her new reality.

It would have seemed to others that her personality found its full expression through her originality with clothes and houses, and to her children she was often an absent or remote parent, yet there was another side. From St Anton in the Austrian Alps, she saw that war was coming, but even after Hitler had annexed the country and marched into Vienna, she stayed on until she had managed to pay off the Swiss border patrol to enable her Jewish friends and acquaintances to take refuge in Switzerland.

Returning to New York in 1940, she and a group of doctors set up a committee for medical and surgical relief to which Millicent devoted herself unstintingly. As its executive chair, she organised the collection of supplies for British field hospitals. When America entered the war, she extended the committee's reach to war-zone hospitals and ships of all the Allied nations. Working her heart to its fragile limit, she extended the collection belt to forty-four states, using all her skills and networks to raise over a million dollars in donations. Later on, according to Millicent's son Arturo, the Medical and Surgical Relief Committee provided a public front for underground operations in five European countries. At its peak the organisation had 600 volunteers.

According to her youngest son Paul, Millicent believed that if you came from a privileged class, your duty and honour came from helping others.[47] She was not interested in recognition and when the French government offered her the Legion of Honour after the war, she declined.

Her health deteriorated while she was living in Virginia in the 1940s, prompting her to take up a new hobby to accommodate her reduced mobility. She had always loved heavy, dramatic jewellery but was finding it increasingly difficult to locate the styles she preferred. Jewellery-making was small enough in scale to be therapeutic for her arthritic fingers and she could sketch her designs and fashion moulds from wax even while bedridden. She could take her tools with her on her travels and sit making her moulds on trains. Her gold jewellery camouflaged and steadied her paralysis. Sometimes she attached a heavy necklace to her bra strap so that it acted like a brace. She drew on nature for her bold designs, featuring dragons and horses as well as stars and flowers. They caught the spirit of American modernity that was sweeping through jewellery design at the time and her pieces quickly became favourites with fashionable women such as Joan Crawford and Dame Edith Sitwell.

A time was coming when her image as a fashion icon would become a yoke from which she must escape. But first there was her most passionate love affair to pass through. Her taste in men had from the beginning reflected her worship of beauty. Starting with an insolvent Austrian count and ending with a troubled Native American war veteran in Taos, all were exceptionally handsome. Unfortunately this territory was cluttered with smooth operators who, with or without money, pursued the pastimes of the rich.

She married three times and during the war conducted affairs with Undersecretary of the US Navy James Forrestal,

British espionage agent Ian Fleming and author Roald Dahl. A few years after divorcing Ronald Balcom, she met Clark Gable, who by then had made his most famous movies, and fell deeply in love. Hollywood had begun to shine as the national centre for glamour and within a year Millicent had decided to follow Gable and move there. The pair became an item and the press predicted marriage, but Clark wasn't good marrying material. One day Millicent found him with another woman. Devastated, she dropped him immediately and fell into a deep depression from which she was aroused only by a visit with friends to New Mexico.

Gilbert Adrian, the leading Hollywood couturier at the time, and his wife Gaynor brought Millicent to Taos, whose queen bee, Mabel Luhan, he had met some years earlier. En route in Santa Fe Millicent saw gorgeous Native American jewellery, blankets, rugs and Spanish colonial artefacts for sale and realised she had stumbled upon a grand new arena for collecting.

Onward to Taos. In 1947 it was still difficult to get there. The mountain gorge could be travelled only by horse or gingerly by car. Millicent came by limo. As the group emerged from the Rio Grande Canyon, a magnificent view opened before them. Across the flat mesa rose Taos Mountain while at its feet lay the pueblo and the town. In the further distance the Sangre de Cristo Mountains stretched across the horizon for as far as the eye could see. Millicent was enthralled; why had no one ever told her about this?

The Adrians took her out to the pueblo. Intuitively she understood that the people's calm serenity was the outward expression of an inner ease with themselves and their environment. They stood apart from material possessions. They just *were*. By this time in her life Millicent was tired of the moneyed social whirl she had always lived in and the Native Americans' way of being offered her an alternative. Up until then she had always, even as a rebel, conformed to the norms of behaviour set by other self-assertive young heiresses. Taos was the untrendiest of places, but it offered something she now very much wanted.

Although Mabel exerted herself to be a good host, Millicent soon wanted a house of her own. Through Mabel she discovered an old adobe building on a thirty-two hectare property. The building, a morada or religious meeting place associated with the Penitente Brotherhood, was tiny, dilapidated and devoid of plumbing, but these drawbacks were eclipsed by magnificent views of Taos Mountain. The house also looked onto meadows of an ever-changing kaleidoscope of colours. Again Millicent had found beauty.

She asked Tony Luhan to provide labour for the work needed and, while waiting for the renovations, stayed at a nearby guest ranch. The lifestyle was informal. Everyone dined together and there were often about fourteen people at the long table. Thornton Wilder was a frequent visitor at the time. Frank Waters came on a regular basis. So did Frieda Lawrence, who had returned to Taos after Lawrence's death, and Brett, whose art had earned increasing admiration. Despite this she had fallen on hard times financially and Millicent went out of her way to help by buying her paintings. Brett introduced Millicent to her friends at the pueblo and accompanied her on shopping trips to Indian markets further afield. Both of them came from high society and loved art and the Native Americans. The eccentricity that had bothered O'Keeffe was of less concern to Millicent. Once when denied a table at a popular restaurant on grounds of inappropriate dress, Brett returned naked but for her fur coat. She loved to tell tall stories about her life in England. And about her mother, who might have been an illegitimate daughter of Napoleon and who threw marbles at Queen Victoria's feet when she wanted to annoy her.

Frieda, Brett and Millicent developed an easy-going friendship. It was acceptable to call on one another without forewarning and no one stood upon ceremony in producing a meal with whatever was at hand. Millicent was delighted to be asked to eat in the kitchen with the others.

Mabel remained outside this circle of three. She admired Millicent's quiet good nature and at first regarded her as a potential friend. She even asked Millicent for her opinion of the Mexican journal she was hoping to publish. Partly she was flattered by Millicent's admiration, 'She loved our house the moment she entered it, she loved me, she loved Tony, she loved Taos. In fact she loved just about everything in the place.'[48] Millicent wasn't pretending. Even back in New York, Mabel's books had inspired her with desire to create a life similar in some respects to Mabel's.

Of course Millicent's take on the life would be different. Inevitably, she found in Taos new inspiration for fashion. The squaw skirt, which sometimes contained rivers of fabric, intrigued her. After trying it out, she got her New York designers to replicate it from fine fabrics according to her own vision. She also modified the short-waisted pueblo jackets, using French velvet and lots of silver buttons. Indian jewellery designs and garments became more widely popular after she wore them in magazine spreads.

Mabel, who was by now sixty-eight, may have found it difficult being outshone by the glamorous forty-five-year-old Millicent, but she really began to resent the newcomer when Tony's interest in her became evident. He saw her often when she was at the guest ranch and even more frequently when she moved into one of Mabel's guesthouses to wait out the remaining period until her house would be ready. As well as seeing her nearly every afternoon at the Big House, he started to call by the guesthouse every day to see how the workers he had provided were getting on and to join them at dinner, which Millicent provided. Sometimes he came home drunk, which infuriated Mabel. He often accompanied Millicent on trips to tribal lands beyond

Taos, making it easier for her to attend dances and ritual performances. Mabel hated his going but tried to moderate her jealousy.

> If only he could continue to love me and not shut me out when he is in this thing with her. And if only this *old fashioned possessiveness* about him would die and cease tormenting me so I could love him purely and unselfishly and *really* be glad for him! That Adam and Eve in us die too hard![49]

Mabel's biographer, Lois Palken Rudnick, believes it is highly unlikely that Millicent's friendship with Tony was a sexual one but their interest in one another was obvious to everyone. When Millicent realised that Mabel was distressed, she asked Frank Waters if he would intercede for her. The idea of her stealing Tony away from Mabel was preposterous, she said, though she later confessed she would have fallen for Tony had she arrived in Taos sooner. She no longer hankered after excessively handsome and flamboyant men; instead she loved Tony's silent serenity and felt she understood him. Frank managed to persuade Mabel not to pursue a divorce, but one day in despondent mood Mabel wrote and told Millicent she didn't want to see her again. Surprised and hurt, Millicent took the letter with her to show Frieda. The talk in the village continued.

Mabel felt the Big House had been poisoned for her and that the only answer was to build another house for herself and Tony. She didn't tell him until the property was bought and plans were well under way. Hill House was to be her last home, where she and Tony would live for most of the rest of their lives. Her torture was resolved only when Tony's young nephew Benito became Millicent's lover and came to live with her in her new home.

There was one way in which Millicent did Mabel a

favour. Mabel reached such a low point that her doctor advised her to write about parts of her life she had long suppressed, including the crippling secret of syphilis that had blighted her married life with Tony. She accepted the doctor's advice, believing that if she undertook this work and wrote it truly, she would be liberated from her pain, 'Work to know, work to tell what you know. Work to find the truth.'[50] In 'The Statue of Liberty', from which Rudnick has quoted liberally now that its long suppression is over, Mabel wrote that she ended sexual relations with Tony after contracting syphilis from him, at last revealing how syphilis affected people of her era. The shame of the disease was so paralysing that at that time she stood alone in the field in writing about it and her memoir is an historically illuminating document.

Out of the pain came something positive for her marriage. Mabel's reflections helped her realise that despite their difficulties, something indissoluble bound her and Tony together, 'More and more the most real and true aspect of our relationship forced itself upon us. We were bound together. We could not break away from each other no matter what we did to each other, no matter what the world did to try to separate us.'[51]

Meanwhile Millicent was having great difficulty translating her vision for Turtle Walk into reality, though she was more exacting with her builders than ever before. Finally the house was expanded from five rooms to eight, but even then it lacked the kind of completion that Millicent had brought to her former homes. This one had a more lived-in look, with ashtrays and books strewn throughout and Indian baskets scattered over the floor. Perhaps that was her way of keeping her mind and spirit open to the transformation offered by Native American spirituality. Brett, whose admiration of Millicent ran to keeping a journal about her life in Taos, helped with the new house. Together they would sit on the floor mixing paint and dreaming up ways to make it beautiful.

Buying whatever she wanted was too big a part of her character for Millicent to jettison. She continued to collect pieces that she liked. Once she saw a necklace that filled her with desire. The man who was wearing it refused to sell, saying he had collected its several hundred pieces of turquoise over many years and polished them himself, but Millicent saw no reason to accept his point of view and within three days a purchase was in hand. In this way she accumulated a massive repository of Indian artefacts and jewellery.

One might wonder whether she had changed at all, but there were a few signs. She no longer sought the kind of men she had once looked for, she turned towards the beauty of earth itself. She loved her final lover, Benito, for the way he looked after her. When she was ill he willingly performed whatever tasks needed to be done.

She treasured the informality of her friendships with Frieda and Brett. Status and prestige counted for much less in her life. The pueblo was a refuge. A visit to the Apache Indian Reservation near Dulce affected her profoundly. She had been excited by extraordinary and beautiful things in Europe and the East but the camp reached into her soul and seemed effortlessly to belong to her. *This*, she declared, was America.

Brett observed Millicent's new happiness. It was clear to her that Millicent felt at home among Native Americans and that their spirit and way of life suited her far better than the life she had led. She liked being simply human without benefit of wealth and rank.

When Millicent learned of the injustices inflicted on Native Americans by successive governments she felt a desire, as she had during the war, to involve herself on their behalf. Believing that the hospital at Taos Pueblo should never have been closed, she funded a delegation of its residents to meet with government officials in Washington, in the hope of getting an Indian health centre on the pueblo. She used her social networks to increase protection and status for Indian art by getting it classified as historic.

Another thing that appalled her was that Native Americans were recorded in government statistics only as numbers and were not entitled to passports. Millicent, along with Frank Waters and others, is thought to have lobbied Washington to grant the Indians full citizenship, but there is no documentation to prove it. The Pueblo custom of keeping no written records probably suited her lack of interest in being lauded for good works.

Towards the end of 1951 she suffered a strep throat which precipitated a steady decline until her death two years later. One of her last excursions was to the Deer Dance at the pueblo. When Brett arrived to pick her up, she found Millicent in a chair, vainly trying to zip up her winter boots. How was she going to manage at the pueblo? Yet once there she walked without help and was able to watch the dance.

Not long before her death, she wrote a last letter to her son Paul, who was then twenty-one, in which she described a moment below Taos Mountain. This letter alone shows how much more she was than a ditsy heiress.

> And I knew that there was no reason to be lonely that one was everything, and Death was as easy as the rising sun and as calm and natural — that to be enfolded in Earth was not an end but part of oneself, part of every day and night that we lived, so that Being part of the Earth one was never alone. And all the fear went out of me — with a great, good stillness and strength.
>
> If anything should happen to me now, ever, just remember all this. I want to be buried in Taos with the wide sky — Life has been marvellous, all the experiences good and bad I have enjoyed, even pain and illness because out of it so many things were discovered. One has

so little time to be still, to lie still and look at the Earth and the changing colours and the Forest — and the voices of people and clouds and light on water, smells and sound and music and the taste of wood smoke in the air.[52]

For the famous New York and Hollywood fashion icon whose last years were a hymn to Indian values and style, it was fitting that Millicent's sons dressed her for burial in an Indian blouse, skirt, moccasins and jewellery, swathed in a Navajo chief's blanket. Mourners from New York and Los Angeles were in attendance and many Native Americans came to the burial, despite their belief that displays of grief or excessive memorials can delay the journey of the departed soul.

After her death, Millicent's sons worked with her friends to create the Millicent Rogers Museum. Paul chose Taos for its location and dedicated most of the rest of his life to its development. At his insistence, a seat on the board of directors was always reserved for the governor of Taos Pueblo. The museum maintains a close connection with the pueblo and gives its staff the day off for San Geronimo Day, the Pueblos' feast day. Once a year the museum invites Pueblo artists to offer their work for sale over a weekend.

The museum was Millicent's legacy to New Mexico, helping people understand and appreciate the beauty and symbolic meaning of many aspects of Native American and Hispanic cultures. Millicent's collection of around 1000 artefacts has blossomed over the last sixty years to reach a 2018 total of over 7000. The Hispanic collection in particular experienced a dramatic growth spurt in the 1980s and Hispanic artists recognise the museum as the first major cultural institution in New Mexico to recognise the significance of the Hispanic art movement.

Sometimes I come away from a museum burdened with a sense of not having done justice to what I have seen. I didn't spend long enough before each item, I didn't understand what I saw, I didn't learn enough, I forgot too much too soon. From the Millicent Rogers Museum I emerged with a feeling of exhilaration. I had seen beauty and it was like hearing music. I could enjoy and be changed by it even without understanding. Millicent's collection has a quality of timeless connection with things of the soul. Beauty was what she did.

12

The Big House
Remembers

The Big House began its long life in 1918 and after a hundred years it is still a refuge of great beauty, a place with a sense of purpose and mission, maintained with loving care and dedication by its owners. A succession of owners put their stamp on it and the many artists, writers, activists, performers and social scientists who have stayed in it have found their creative energies released or transformed.

For Mabel the houses she lived in became a canvas on which to paint her passage towards enlightenment, aiming, as she wrote in her memoir *Intimate Memories*, to reveal 'the natural growth of a personality struggling to become individual, growing through all degrees of crudity to a greater sophistication and on to simplicity'.[53]

John Collier's son remembered the Big House as mysterious and magical, full of blazing colour, the heavy furniture contrasting with 'exquisite, tactile pillows and curtains'. It added up, he thought, echoing Mabel's own assessment, to 'an extension of her interior design'.[54]

From 1918 until Mabel died in 1962, the Big House provided a meeting place for her chosen — people likely to change America for the better. It was a haven for artists, writers, photographers, reformers and students of humanity. It offered an alternative way of living and of seeing. Some, such as D H Lawrence, Carl Jung and Dorothy Brett, crossed oceans to get there. The majority hailed from New York or California. Many had met before, but the Big House provided a place for cross-fertilisation of ideas in a landscape that gave a different perspective to humanity's place on earth.

For many, the experience was life-changing. Mabel was described in an early 1920s Chicago newspaper as 'the most peculiar common denominator that society, literature, art and radical revolutionaries ever found in New York and Europe'. Her reach was astonishing and so was the range and quality of work produced by her protégés and visitors. In the words of Ansel Adams, whose own career achieved clearer definition in Taos, she had 'talons for talent'.

Talons is right, for Mabel wasn't all sweetness and giving. She was also ego and entitlement, restlessness and tumultuous emotion. She tried to exact loyalty on her own terms. Mabel saw many of her male visitors as people damaged by mother–son relationships. She once declared, 'And really when all these mother complexes sat down with me at my table this summer I couldn't eat a thing — it was so tense!'[55]

Gilbert Adrian, the Hollywood clothes designer who brought Millicent Rogers to Taos in the late 1940s, found that Mabel used her generosity with the Big House to seduce her visitors into revealing their most intimate secrets. Perhaps it was this that induced many of her male visitors to prescribe death for Mabel-characters in their fiction. Rudnick catches the melodrama perfectly,

Mabel has been imagined dead in a greater variety of ways than any other woman in American literary history. She has been disposed of by gang rape and suicide, had her heart torn out in an Indian sacrificial ritual, been squeezed to death by a snake and blinded by a vulture. By her own hand, in *Water of Life*, she froze to death on a mountain top. None of these deaths, however, matches her apocalyptic finale in Myron Brinig's *All of Their Lives*, in which she is struck dead by a stroke of heaven-sent lightning as she gallops furiously across the most precipitous mountain peak in New Mexico.[56]

Yet for all their vitriol, many maintained affection for Mabel and at least on-again off-again relationships with her. A few, like Frank Waters and Thornton Wilder, who visited often in the 1930s, simply liked her. Waters always defended her and his sympathies during the gathering intensity of Millicent Rogers' relationship with Tony seemed to be mainly with Mabel.

The Southwest was a landmass that drew women of strong life-force, strong creativity, who wanted to invent for themselves a way of being that was not defined by men. In an unpublished play, the African American poet and spiritual leader Jean Toomer noted that it was women who were claiming the stark, isolated man's country of New Mexico.

But, like the men, female visitors also reacted with ambivalence towards Mabel. For Mary Austin, who stayed at the Big House before setting up her permanent home in Santa Fe, Mabel, Tony and the Big House became a stabilising anchor but she needed to live at arm's length in Santa Fe. She was disparaging about Mabel's artistic and writerly achievements and in her 1931 novel *Starry Adventure* she satirised her and the Big House. The Mabel-character, Eudora Ballantine, creates a home in which she throws together different periods and styles. She collects people for the purpose of adding them to her collection of indigenous items. The Hispanic aristocrat whom she marries endows her restored villa with the finishing touch.

The greatest gift of the Big House was arguably Tony Luhan. He willingly used his contacts to help visitors gain access to Taos Pueblo and Native American populations further afield, acting as chauffeur and interpreter of the customs and spirituality of a very private people. He became a loyal supporter of some of the ethnographers and what they wrote, helping to offset criticism from the Pueblo.

Though some of the men mocked him for his vanity, the female visitors spoke of him in glowing terms. O'Keeffe in particular mentioned the importance of Tony in her letters to Stieglitz. Without him her experience of New Mexico would have been much less profound. To Millicent Rogers and others he offered an alternative model of manhood — tender, understanding, accepting. It was not easy to be a female artist or creator of any kind in the America they hailed from. Men defined what art was, what its suitable subjects were and how they should be presented. Brett probably said it for them all when she wrote of Taos, 'Gradually I began to emerge, to realise the freedom, the expansion, of living. I began to find myself, my place and later a purpose.'[57]

Tony paid a price, however, for his relationship with Mabel, losing his ranking as head of his clan through his neglect of tribal duties, and he was progressively shut out of his tribe's religious ceremonies.

In many cases a stay at the Big House heralded a change in career or focus. Ansel Adams and Edward Weston were excited to be in a place where the sky mattered. O'Keeffe allowed the land to seep into her bones. John Marin's cloud watching transformed his watercolours during his two summers at the Big House.

The adobe of which the Big House was built fitted the landscape perfectly. Its picturesque beauty was only enhanced by the modern conveniences and comfort of arrangements within. Inside the adobe dwellings at the pueblos, however, poverty and hardship often reigned. For the visitors to the Big House seeking something different and more hopeful, more spiritually satisfying than the places they came from, it was all too easy for wish-fulfilment to define their perceptions. Adobe was charming, the Indians were leaders in wisdom and spirituality, the landscapes were majestic reminders of man's dependence. There was no place in this scenario for the poverty hidden by adobe, the health problems of overcrowding, the scars of mining and forestry.

In addition, the Native Americans were innocent victims of the Spanish conquest and US federal law and it was easy not to notice that Hispanos too had suffered. Their grazing lands decreased when half the public domain was allocated to the National Forest and again as a result of the land claims work pressed by Mabel, John Collier, Mary Austin and others in the 1920s. Their inattention to Hispanic perceptions and realities helped aggravate tensions with Native Americans.

These effects were never the intention of the visitors to the Big House, who were generally kind-hearted and motivated to be a force for good. Many made efforts to help improve the wellbeing of the native people. Indirectly they helped create markets for the art and crafts of both Native Americans and Hispanos.

The visitors came, they saw, they to some extent misrepresented. It's the classic colonial story. Even when well intentioned, colonisers reduced the native population of their adopted country to a set of stereotypes in the service of what they called the 'mother culture'. Embedded in a culture of progress and deliberate exploitation, they rarely transcended those confines. But even without colonialism, humanity seems to be hardwired to see people in terms of in-group and other, a situation that has a natural tendency to encourage prejudice and cruelty. Yet the visitors to the Big House possessed a genuine desire to appreciate Native American culture and the uncompromising grandeur and beauty of the land. Their efforts added much to American enlightenment.

And the story continues. After Mabel's death, the Big House went into a new phase of existence. First came family members, then in 1970 it was bought by Dennis Hopper, who had been to Taos and seen the house during filming of *Easy Rider*, which he directed. Mabel had hoped that future owners would continue her vision for it as a retreat for movers and shakers. Hopper was a mover and shaker of a kind and as a delinquent in the style of his mentor James Dean he had a kind of dystopian vision, but it could not have been further from Mabel's. He believed the art of creation was inextricably linked to the art of destruction. With his discerning eye for art, he built up an impressive collection by modern artists such as Andy Warhol and many of them came to visit at the Big House, but the art of those he was closest to featured the annihilation of the world.

His was the first generation to grow up with the reality that the entire world could be annihilated by an atom bomb. As children they had been taught to hide under their desks in the advent of a nuclear detonation and had seen their parents build bomb shelters in their gardens. For the second time, a wave of young people was on the run from mainstream American culture, but these juniors were far less equipped than their predecessors to succeed in joining the existing cultures of New Mexico or to make any kind of living in the third poorest state in the union. Economically the hippies were a threat to the Hispanos, taking their low-paid jobs and inflating land values. Promiscuous sex and abundance of drug use were anathema to Hispanic values and the hippies were blamed when drug use in schools as well as hepatitis and venereal disease began to rise. Local business people put up signs such as 'We will refuse service to anyone we consider a health menace' or 'Keep America Beautiful, Take a Hippie to a Carwash'. The hippies favoured Native Americans over Hispanic people and their values and during 1970 things took a violent turn. Hippies' cars were burned and dynamited; they themselves were beaten and pistol-whipped. New Mexico was far from the idyll they had imagined. The Native Americans of Taos Pueblo were preoccupied with their Blue Lake case and remained largely outside the conflict.

Came Hopper into the mix. He fell in love with Taos and couldn't leave. Here was a chance to live out his rebellious nature and also to explore mystical beliefs and practices he was strongly attracted to. The adobe Mabel had lovingly sourced from the earth now formed the basis of Hopper's 'Mud Palace' and initially the Big House was in danger of being violated by a neon sign to flash home the point, but on the whole Hopper wanted the place to retain its original character. He followed up on the history of the house, even visiting the cave used by Lawrence as the setting for the human sacrifice of his Mabel-character in 'The Woman Who Rode Away'.

Hopper hoped to rival Mabel's achievement by having as many influential people pass through it in his time as she had in hers. During his nine years there he ticked off such as the Everly Brothers, Bob Dylan, Kris Kristofferson, Leonard Cohen, Alan Watts, John Wayne, Peter Fonda and Jack Nicholson, but few stayed very long or seemed to have been deeply inspired by the Big House or the landscape. Los Alamos made a greater impact. Artists like Tony Price were inspired by its malevolent purpose to create symbols of peace from its obsolete weaponry. He transformed some hydrogen bomb castings into evocations of Tibetan gongs, which Hopper installed on Mabel's summer porch. Price often named these works after gods and myths.

Dorothy Brett, who had spent more time living on the premises than any of the creatives of Mabel's generation, was very upset when Hopper bought the Big House, but in time she and Georgia O'Keeffe enjoyed recounting stories of the old days to Hopper and his friends. Brett, whom they appreciated as the last of the Great Bohemians, told a Hopperesque anecdote about Lawrence turning into a coyote after taking too much peyote. She recounted how, baring both flesh and teeth, he had to be chained up in Mabel's courtyard, where he howled the night out.

Hopper surrounded himself at the Big House with a group of people to help edit *The Last Movie*, which he hoped would finally expose the empty illusions adulated in ordinary films. A few filmmakers positioned Hopper as their 'great white hope' who would make connections between middle-class Anglos, Hollywood and local people, but Hopper was too much at the mercy of his demons and too lacking in sensitivity to others to be able to accomplish anything much. He fell back on weaponry. Soon after his arrival, he got into an argument and pulled a gun. After his release from gaol, he and his friends bought up every rifle and semi-automatic they could find in Taos. By Hopper's own admission, the Big House became an armed encampment. Rudnick spoke to visitors who remembered gun patrols on the roof and security guards communicating on walkie-talkies.[58]

Bothered by the hostility of local people, Hopper bought a cinema where he showed free Disney cartoons at weekends and he helped teach local Hispanos about filmmaking. He also helped raise funds for the Blue Lake. But the community never accepted him. It didn't want him or the people he brought with him.

And then there were the ghosts. People walked and talked in Mabel's room when no one was there, doors opened and shut, chairs moved, door knobs jiggled. When Dennis's guests overindulged in drugs and drink and started to abuse Mabel, paintings flew off the walls onto their heads; Tony and local Indians also haunted the house. Frank Waters suggested burning copal to get rid of the ghosts but it didn't work.

Apart from the presence of the dead, there was the presence of the living to contend with. There were so many of those that when Hopper came downstairs to get something out of the fridge, he would find thirty people milling around whom he had never seen before. To Where's the orange juice? they'd answer, Who are you?[59] However, when he sold the Big House in 1977, he said of his sojourn there that it was the first time he'd felt he had a home. He stayed on in Taos, renting the Tony House but sinking into insanity. Drug-induced hallucinations brought him visions of Lawrence's ghost wandering the grounds. In one respect he had surpassed Lawrence, making the proud boast that whereas Lawrence had lived in Taos for nine months, he had lived there for nine years. In 1985 there was a sea change in the way he was able to handle his past and a year later he moved to California, taking Mabel's dining table with him.

The next owners of the Big House were people with dreams more akin to Mabel's, but with an educational rather than an artistic focus. Kitty and George Otero were of a sixties generation that prized community, ethnic diversity, peace and genuine democracy. As an Hispano, George wanted to help improve his people's standing in the nation. The couple yearned for a society in which personal growth and social responsibility went hand in hand. They developed educational programmes that could help achieve the dream. They changed the name of the Big House to Las Palomas — the doves — and named their programme after it.

At first there was local resistance. The Big House had a reputation for being a home for crackpots, but when the

Oteros began securing large grants their local credibility improved. During the following decade they brought to Taos over 40,000 students, teachers and other visitors.

What Kitty found out about Mabel was to her a turn-off. The woman was 'so horrible' Kitty couldn't bear to tell people about her, yet the ambience of the Big House was pivotal to the success of the venture. George wanted the programme to be a home away from home where people could reflect in a safe, tranquil environment.

The Oteros also played a crucial role in a reform movement that took place in schools in the late 1970s. An important thrust of this movement was to develop school management along democratic lines, with meaningful participation by students, and the Big House was central to the training and development involved. With Los Alamos never far from people's minds, many of the conferences and workshops tackled issues of war. As economic inequality was understood to be another threat to peaceful human coexistence, the students played out the closing of an auto plant in Detroit and its removal to Brazil. Subsequently, many found creative ways in their home towns and schools of consolidating the vision of Las Palomas. One group set up a world affairs conference for their school in Denver; another helped organise a conference of 1000 youth in Chicago; and a California group persuaded its community to ban the use of Styrofoam.

The Big House was recognised as a national special-issue centre with responsibility for developing connections between global issues and community education. However, such programmes were expensive to run, and maintenance of the Big House, which was now a nationally registered historic home, was an ongoing problem. The property entered a phase of going on and off the market at regular intervals.

Came Jenny Robin Jones. By then the Big House was an inn and conference centre. The o-m had heard of it through a friend and we were intrigued by its connections with Lawrence, Cather and O'Keeffe. The o-m liked the house well enough but to me it seemed to possess some special magic, some spiritual promise. I was excited in a way I had not felt in years. As to why, I had no idea, but the adrenalin was pulsing through my veins and my attention was intensely focussed.

On my first day at the house, a group came to hear about Mabel's life and on my last a novelist came to write about her ghost. The personality of Mabel Dodge Luhan began to infiltrate my psyche. I had long been a student of literature and the arts, so on my return to New Zealand, I followed up the Lawrence thread, then the Cather thread and then the O'Keeffe thread. I discovered Frank Waters and Millicent Rogers. By the end of my studies, I felt connected with America and its history in a way that, surely, could be communicated to others.

Epilogue

When I began this book I wondered how much of my relationship with the o-m it would include. As it happened, our relationship ended a couple of months after our return and I had no wish to expose sensitive personal areas to a general readership. For several months after the relationship ended, we had no contact. Then we began meeting for lunch on a regular basis and I told the o-m I wanted to write a book about the trip. He was delighted but serious.

> You must write whatever you need to. I don't want you to consider my feelings at all. I think you have been too often held back in your writing out of concern for the feelings of those you may write about.

He had given such careful thought to the progress of my writing and to how he could set me free. I saw he felt o-m!

intensely about this. Still, I had decided I didn't need to write deeply about our relationship and I saw no reason to change.

All through our trip the o-m and I had conducted our intellectual explorations, exhilarating each other and filling our journey with meaning and progress. Yet all the while there was that physical coldness, our inability to reach out to one another with our bodies, the o-m's inability to hug and say I love you. Seemingly unfixable, our reliance on intellect distorted our relationship and his quick surrender to anger, which I had experienced over Joan Didion, seemed to kill the possibility of love. Twin beds, sustained politeness. Let's talk about America.

As the story of the world became harder and harder to bring under a canopy of belief in progressive enlightenment, as Trump came in and strongmen seemed to rule the world, taking us faster and faster towards environmental catastrophe, I had a feeling I must love America or despair.

The Alt-u?

I learned to imagine America *without* its Westerners — to see, in wholeness and freedom, coyotes, snakes, cactus, geology, plains, mountains, rivers, Native Americans. Then I reconstructed the country by learning its historical evolution, then I put the Westerners back in. And today, in its piteous wake of Covid-19 devastation, I embrace it in its entirety, glorying especially in its fabulous commentators, its intelligentsia, its novels, poetry and art, its belief in the possibility of the betterment of humankind.

I had been writing this book for a couple of years when a mutual friend told me the o-m was dying. He had been diagnosed with bladder cancer and had not long to live. I had emailed him the week before about lunch but received no answer, so I rang and found the news was true. We arranged to meet for lunch the following week. On the day, the o-m rang me to say he could not make it to town, so I took some sandwiches over to his place. We talked about his illness and how he felt about dying. He was not afraid, he accepted that his time had come.

The next time I rang, his sister-in-law answered the phone. She was staying there now, she said, because he needed someone with him 24/7. I went over that afternoon. The change was shocking. The o-m was in bed asleep, his face so thin I had to decipher the man I'd known. His whole body seemed shrunk to bone. He would take no food, only water. I whispered, 'It's Jenny.' He opened his eyes and smiled. I knew he was delighted to see me. I took his hand and held it. He said how wonderful it was to touch. He indicated I should entwine my fingers within his because that way he could feel the touch better.

We sat quietly together and then I told him the plan I had conceived on the bus. 'You know the book I'm writing about our trip to the States?' He nodded. 'I want to dedicate it to you.' He opened his eyes fully and the pressure on my fingers increased. 'Oh, I never envisaged (still using a word like that), I never envisaged . . .' He kept referring to my gift, his tone raised like an incantation, 'The dedication . . . the dedication.' It seemed an embarrassingly small thing to me, this little gift of love, a dedication in a book that might never be finished, might never be published. But to him, I saw, it was something set in stone, entirely solid, a thing that could not be taken away and would still be there when he was dead.

The o-m was a humble man who, though he had many friends, had not dared presume upon their affection. During our relationship he had not expressed emotion easily but now it flowed unimpeded and I saw he felt replete. It was as if in these moments his world became something he had not dared hope for.

Then he grew sad and murmured in his new slurred way, 'It's all wasted. This marvellous experience is all wasted because I'll never be able to write it. As a *writer* it is wasted.' I could not bear it. I said, 'I won't be able to write it as you would write it but I'll — I'll try to write it.'

I knew I was making a promise I might not be able to fulfil, but he was satisfied. 'You will. You will.' All the power in his body went into those words. Then his head, temporarily raised, fell back on the pillow.

As I left I said, 'I love you,' and he responded, 'Oh, I love you, Jenny. It's marvellous loving you.' I often thought of that afterwards, wondering at the way all this came about and what it signified about what had gone before. As he lay dying, he was fully there, fully able to express his feelings. How sad that it could not be said before. While we were in the States perhaps. New Mexico. Taos. The Willa Cather Room.

Our goodbye felt like a healing of all the difficulties in our relationship. I felt I saw the o–m whole for the first time and suddenly I found that my reluctance to write about our relationship had evaporated. Suddenly my attitude to writing the book changed from one of steady, slow, incremental progress to one of exhilarated, intense involvement. Suddenly I was eager to get up in the morning and get to my desk each day. It felt as though the o–m was with me and at my shoulder, urging me onward. The book had become a way of honouring and deepening our relationship.

In the end I realised the book did not call for a deep exposition of our relationship. The o–m had given it his blessing and left it to me to decide, and that was what mattered.

Acknowledgements & Permissions

As always, thanks are due to those who have gone before, those who wrote and recorded the history and shared their knowledge. Especially to Lois Palken Rudnick for her immensely thorough and insightful books about Mabel Dodge Luhan and the artists' colony in Taos.

On a personal level, heartfelt thanks to Linda Cassells, who has been so much more than a publisher to me, offering a sharp mind and generous encouragement along the way. And to my partner Brian for his unflagging enthusiasm to support me in everything I do.

Apart from these two, the writing this time has been mostly an act of solitude. Apart, that is, from a burst of intensive correspondence around the seeking of permission to quote copyrighted material. The task of discovering where copyright lies and then of obtaining permission is full of difficulty. As the concept of fair use is not pin-downable in any concrete way except as determined in a court of law and as the publisher and I opted for certainty rather than 'likely fair use', it was a long and sometimes unsuccessful journey. The most crippling difficulty was waiting for many weeks for world rights only to learn that the rights on offer were limited to the US and Canada, and that permission would need to be sought elsewhere for the UK and Commonwealth, requiring another wait of up to ten weeks. If the system for locating copyright holders is not actually broken it is resolutely Dickensian.

But the reason I'm including these comments here is that many of my correspondents went out of their way to be helpful. Such kindness was what kept me going. In particular I'd like to thank Edith Sandler at the Library of Congress, Stacy Lunsford at the University of New Mexico, Sally Welch at Ohio University Press, Carmela Quinto at the Millicent Rogers Museum and Tori Duggan and Rana Chan at the Georgia O'Keeffe Museum.

With thanks to the following for permission to quote excerpts:

The Man Who Killed the Deer by Frank Waters
Copyright © 1942, 1970
By permission of Ohio University Press,
www.ohioswallow.com.

Bibliography &
Further Reading

Abbreviations

MDLC: Mabel Dodge Luhan Collection, Yale Collection of American Literature, Beinecke Rare Book and Manuscript Library
UNM: University of New Mexico Press, Albuquerque, New Mexico

List of books

Alinder, Mary Street, *Ansel Adams: A Biography*. Bloomsbury, New York, 2014.

Archbishop Lamy: In His Own Words, translated and edited by Thomas J. Steele, S.J. LPD Press, Albuquerque, 2000.

Bachrach, Arthur J., *D.H. Lawrence in New Mexico — the time is different there*. University of New Mexico Press, Albuquerque, 2006.

Bingham, Sallie, *Cory's Feast*. Sunstone Press, Santa Fe, 2005.

Brett, Dorothy, *Lawrence and Brett: A Friendship*. Sunstone Press, Santa Fe, 2006.

Brooke, Sylvia, *Queen of the Headhunters: The Autobiography of H.H. the Hon Sylvia Brooke, Ranee of Sarawak*. Sidgwick & Jackson, London, 1970.

Burns, Cherie, *Searching for Beauty: The Life of Millicent Rogers, the American Heiress Who Taught the World about Style*. Griffin imprint, St Martin's Press, New York, 2012.

Cline, Lynn, *Literary Pilgrims: The Santa Fe and Taos Writers' Colonies 1917–1950*. University of New Mexico Press, Albuquerque, 2007.

Cather, Willa, *Death Comes for the Archbishop*. First published 1927. This edition Vintage Classics, New York, 1990.

Cather, Willa, *O Pioneers!*, 1913. This edition Hesperus Press Ltd, London, 2013.

————, *My Antonia*, 1918. This edition Houghton Mifflin Company, Boston, 1988.

————, *Not Under Forty*. Cassell, London, 1936.

Conant, Jennet, *109 East Palace: Robert Oppenheimer and the Secret City of Los Alamos*. Simon and Schuster, New York, 2006.

de Aragon, Ray John, *Padre Martinez and Bishop Lamy*. Sunstone Press, Santa Fe, 2006.

Dyer, Geoff, *Out of Sheer Rage: In the Shadow of D.H. Lawrence*. Canongate

Books, Edinburgh, 2015.

Georgia O'Keefe, edited by Tanya Barson. Abrams, New York, 2016.

Gibson, Carrie, *El Norte: The Epic and Forgotten Story of Hispanic North America*. Grove Atlantic, New York, 2019.

Hawthorne, Nathaniel, *The Scarlet Letter: A Romance*. Ticknor Reed & Fields, Boston, 1850.

Lawrence, D H, *Mornings in Mexico and Other Essays*, edited by Virginia Crosswhite Hyde. Cambridge University Press, Cambridge, 2009.

_____, *Phoenix: The Posthumous Papers of D.H. Lawrence* (1936). Viking Press, New York, 1972.

_____, *The Plumed Serpent*, William Heinemann Ltd. First published 1926, this edition 1965.

_____, *The Woman Who Rode Away/St Mawr/The Princess*. 1925 and 1928, this edition Penguin Classics, London, 2006.

_____, *Selected Essays*, introduced by Richard Aldington. Penguin Books, London, 1950.

_____, *Studies in Classic American Literature*. First published by William Heinemann 1924, this Penguin edition, Middlesex, 1971.

Lewis, Edith, *Willa Cather Living: A Personal Record*. University of Nebraska Press, Lincoln, 1953, this edition 2000.

Lynes, Barbara Buhler, Poling-Kempes, Lesley and Turner, Fredrick W, *Georgia O'Keeffe and New Mexico: A Sense of Place*. Georgia O'Keefe Museum, Santa Fe, and Princeton University Press, New Jersey, 2004.

Luhan, Mabel Dodge, *Lorenzo in Taos*. Alfred Knopf, New York, 1932.

_____, *Edge of Taos Desert: an escape to reality*. UNM, 1937.

_____, *Winter in Taos*. Harcourt, Brace and Company, New York, 1935.

My Faraway One: Selected Letters of Georgia O'Keeffe and Alfred Stieglitz: Volume One, 1915–1933, edited by Sarah Greenough. Yale University Press, New Haven, Connecticut, 2011.

New Mexican Lives: Profiles and Historical Stories, edited by Richard W. Etulain. University of New Mexico Press, Albuquerque, 2002.

Padre Martinez: New Perspectives from Taos, Essays by E.A. Mares, Bette S. Weidman, Thomas J. Steele, S.J., Patricia Clark Smith, Ray John de Aragon. Millicent Rogers Museum, Taos, New Mexico, 1988.

Reily, Nancy Hopkins, *Georgia O'Keeffe: A Private Friendship, Part 11 Walking the Abiquiu and Ghost Ranch Land*. Sunstone Press, Santa Fe, 2009.

Rudnick, Lois Palken, *Mabel Dodge Luhan, New Woman, New Worlds*. UNM,

Albuquerque, 1984.

———————— (ed.), *The Suppressed Memoirs of Mabel Dodge Luhan: Sex, Syphilis, and Psychoanalysis in the Making of Modern American Culture*. UNM, Albuquerque, 2012.

————————, *Utopian Vistas: the Mabel Dodge Luhan House and the American Counterculture*. UNM, Albuquerque, 1996, first paperbound printing, 1998.

Terra Incognita: D.H. Lawrence at the Frontiers, edited by Virginia Crosswhite Hyde and Earl G. Ingersoll. Fairleigh Dickinson University Press, Rosemont Publishing & Printing Corp., 2010.

The Selected Letters of Willa Cather, edited by Andrew Jewell and Janis Stout. Alfred A. Knopf, New York, 2013.

Waters, Frank, *Brave are My People: Indian Heroes not Forgotten*. Clear Light Publishers, Santa Fe, 1993.

————————, *The Man Who Killed the Deer*. Neville Spearman Ltd, 1942. This edition Swallow Press, Ohio University Press, Athens, 1962.

————————, *The Woman at Otowi Crossing*. First published 1966. This edition Swallow Press/Ohio University Press, Athens, 1997.

Articles

'D.H. Lawrence and the American Indians' by Jeffery Meyers, *Michigan Quarterly Review*, Vol. 56, Issue 2, Spring 2017 accessed on 15 May 2020 at http://hdl.handle.net/2027/spo.act2080.0056.221.

'Going to Lawrence for feeling: A Study of "The Princess"' by Natalya Reinhold in *Etudes Lawrenciennes*, No 43, 2012, p. 203–214, accessed on 10 March 2020 at https://journals.openedition.org/lawrence/99.

'I Interact, Therefore, I Am: LaDonna Harris and the Return of Taos Blue Lake' by Ashley Sherry, accessed on 27 September 2018 at http://newmexicohistory.org/people/i-interact-therefore-i-am-ladonna-harris-and-the-return-of-taos-blue-lake.

'Now I Have Become Death: Picturing the Bomb' by Dr. Jeanne S.M. Willette in *Art History Unstuffed*, 16 August 2014, accessed on 30 July 2019 at http://arthistoryunstuffed.com/now-i-have-become-death-picturing-the-bomb.

'The $44m for Georgia O'Keeffe's work shows how little female artists are valued', Jonathan Jones, *The Guardian*, 21 November 2014.

Images

For anyone interested in seeing paintings and photographs relating to people and places mentioned in this book, please visit Jenny Robin Jones on Pinterest. Images of O'Keeffe paintings, The Big House, Mabel Dodge and Tony Luhan, Taos Pueblo, Millicent Rogers, Frank Waters, Padre Martinez and Bishop Lamy can of course be found at the websites of galleries such as Tate Modern, the Georgia O'Keeffe Museum and generally all over the internet.

You may also like to visit the author at jennyrobinjones.com.

References

1 Cather, Willa, *The Song of the Lark*, Houghton Mifflin, Boston, 1915, p. 368.

2 *Queen of the Headhunters, The Autobiography of H.H. the Hon. Sylvia Brooke, Ranee of Sarawak*, Sidgwick & Jackson, London, 1970.

3 *The Letters of D. H. Lawrence*, ed. George J. Zytaruk and James T. Boulton, Cambridge University Press, 2002, Vol. 2, p. 417.

4 Luhan, Mabel Dodge, *Lorenzo in Taos*, Alfred A. Knopf, New York, 1932, p. 3. Cited in Rudnick, *Utopian Vistas: The Mabel Dodge Luhan House and the American Counterculture*, UNM, 1996, p. 99.

5 Letter: Maurice Sterne to Luhan, November 1917. Cited in Rudnick, *Mabel Dodge Luhan: New Woman, New Worlds*, UNM, p. 142.

6 Luhan, Mabel Dodge, *Edge of Taos Desert: An Escape to Reality*, first edition 1937, this edition UNM, 1987, p. 275.

7 Ibid., p. 62.

8 Ibid., p. 291.

9 These writings were published in a literary magazine, *The Dial*, prior to publication of *Sea and Sardinia* in December 1921.

10 D H Lawrence, *Phoenix: The Posthumous Papers*, ed. Edward McDonald, Heinemann, London, 1936, p. 90.

11 Luhan, Mabel Dodge, *Lorenzo in Taos*, Alfred A. Knopf, New York, 1932, p. 10. Cited in Rudnick, *Mabel Dodge Luhan*, p. 199.

12 Lawrence, D H, *The Plumed Serpent*, William Heinemann Ltd, 1926, this edition 1965, p. 388.

13 Lawrence, D H, 'St Mawr'. First published 1925. Cited in *The Woman Who Rode Away/St. Mawr/The Princess*, Penguin Classics, London, 2006, p. 76.

14 Ibid., p. 111.

15 Ibid., p. 120.

16 *The Letters of D H Lawrence*, Vol. 5. 1924–1927. Ed. James T. Boulton and Lindeth Vasey, Cambridge University Press, Cambridge, 1989.

17 'An Appeal by the Pueblo Indians of New Mexico to the People of the United States', 5 November 1922. Found in the *John Collier Papers*, Reel 8. The statement was signed by Taos, San Juan, Santa Clara, San Ildefonso, Nambe, Tesuque, Cochiti, Santo Domingo, San Filipe, Santa Ana, Zia, Jemez, Pecos, Sandia, Isleta, Laguna, Acoma, Picuris, Pojoaque, and Zuni pueblos. Cited in: *The Bursum Bill and the Pueblo Lands Board Act: Culture, Law, and Politics in the Borderlands of the American Southwest* by Bobby Edwards and Dr. Daniel Widener, UCSD, Spring 2017.

18 Rudnick, *Mabel Dodge Luhan*, p. 215.

19 Waters, Frank, *The Man Who Killed the Deer*, Swallow Press/Ohio University Press, Athens, 1942, this edition 1970, p. 170.

20 Ibid., p. 63.

21 Ibid., p. 80.

22 Ibid., p. 244.

23 Ibid., p. 174.

24 'I Interact, Therefore, I Am: LaDonna Harris and the Return of Taos Blue Lake' by Ashley Sherry, accessed on 27 September 2018 at http://newmexicohistory.org/people/i-interact-therefore-i-am-ladonna-harris-and-the-return-of-taos-blue-lake.

25 Waters, Frank, *The Woman at Otowi Crossing*, Swallow Press/Ohio University Press, Athens, 1966, this edition 1987, p. vii.

26 Wikipedia, accessed 1 December 2019 at https://en.wikipedia.org/wiki/Trinity_(nuclear_test).

27 Ibid.

28 Waters, *The Woman at Otowi Crossing*, p, 21.

29 Ibid., p. 204.

30 Ibid., p. 207.

31 Weidman, Bette S., 'Willa Cather's Art in Historical Perspective: Reconsidering Death Comes for the Archbishop', in *Padre Martinez: New Perspectives from Taos*, Millicent Rogers Museum, Taos, 1988, p. 63.

32 O'Keeffe, Georgia in Exhibition Catalogue, 'An American Place', 1939.

33 Letter to Mabel Dodge Luhan, MDLC, New York, 1925.

34 Rudnick, *Mabel Dodge Luhan*, p. 235.

35 Rudnick, *Utopian Vistas*, p. 139.

36 Ibid., p. 136.

37 Luhan, 'Family Affairs' memoir. Cited in Rudnick, *Suppressed Memoirs of Mabel Dodge Luhan: Sex, Syphilis, and Psychoanalysis in the Making of Modern American Culture*, UNM, 2012, p. 112.

38 Ibid., in Rudnick, *Suppressed Memoirs*, p. 113.

39 Ibid., in Rudnick, *Suppressed Memoirs*, p. 115.

40 Ibid., in Rudnick, *Suppressed Memoirs*, p. 109.

41 Ibid., in Rudnick, *Suppressed Memoirs*, p. 116.

42 Rudnick, Lois Palken, *Mabel Dodge Luhan*, p. 239.

43 'Now I Have Become Death: Picturing the Bomb' by Dr. Jeanne S.M.Willette in *Art History Unstuffed*, 16 August 2014, accessed on 30 July 2019 at arthistoryunstuffed.com/now-i-have-become-death-picturing-the-bomb.

44 Hollis, Janet. 'Two American Women in Art — O'Keeffe and Cassatt', *Delphian Quarterly*, 28 April 1945: 15.

45 Jones, Jonathan, 'The $44m for Georgia O'Keeffe's work shows how little female artists are valued', *The Guardian*, 21 November 2014.

46 Luhan, 'The Doomed' memoir. Cited in Rudnick, *Suppressed Memoirs*, p. 177.

47 Burns, Cherie, *Searching for Beauty: The Life of Millicent Rogers, the American Heiress Who Taught the World about Style*, St Martin's Griffin, New York, 2011, p. 299.

48 Luhan, 'The Statue of Liberty' memoir. Cited in Rudnick, *Suppressed Memoirs*, p. 170.

49 Ibid., in Rudnick, *Suppressed Memoirs*, p. 168.

50 Ibid., in Rudnick, *Suppressed Memoirs*, p. 127.

51 Ibid., in Rudnick, *Suppressed Memoirs*, p. 128.

52 Letter from Millicent Rogers to her youngest son Paul Peralta-Ramos, 1952. Held by Millicent Rogers Museum, Taos.

53 Luhan, *Intimate memories: Background*, Harcourt, Brace, New York, 1933, p.16. Cited in Rudnick, *Utopian Vistas*, p. 49.

54 Rudnick, *Utopian Vistas*, p. 44–5.

55 Rudnick, *Mabel Dodge Luhan*, p. 199.

56 Ibid., p. 302.

57 Rudnick, *Utopian Vistas*, p. 117

58 Ibid., p. 255.

59 Ibid., p. 258.

Index